CROATIA

HISTORY · CULTURE · ART HERITAGE

Written, edited and designed by
ANTUN TRAVIRKA

Photographs by
ŽIVKO BAČIĆ
MARIO BELIĆ
ANDRIJA CARLI
RENCO KOSINOŽIĆ
MLADEN RADOLOVIĆ
DAVOR ŠARIĆ
GORAN VRANIĆ
NIKOLA VRANIĆ
VELID JAKUPOVIĆ
ŠIME FABRIS

Editor-in-Chief and Responsible Editor
ĐURĐICA ŠOKOTA

For the Publisher
ŽIVKO ŠOKOTA

Translated by
STIPE GRGAS

© FORUM - ZADAR, 2018.

ISBN 978-953-179-925-6

CIP zapis dostupan u računalnom katalogu
Nacionalne i sveučilišne knjižnice u Zagrebu
pod brojem 633467

CROATIA

HISTORY · CULTURE · ART HERITAGE

ANTUN TRAVIRKA

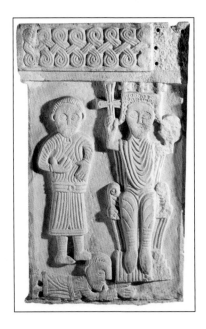

FORUM

Zelenjak nearby Klanjec, a monument to the Croatian national anthem on the site which inspired its composer Antun Mihanović

Left: Velebit, the stream Paklenica

When at the dawn of Croatian Romanticism the poet Antun Mihanović wrote his poem «Croatian Homeland» which, amongst other Illyrian patriotic songs, was published in 1835 in the famous journal «Danica» it was even then recognized as a wholly singular expression of love of country and patriotism. In its originally seven two stanza fragments, instead of the then usual bombastic style, the poem succeeded, in a poetically convincing and Romantically exalted manner, to condense the sense of the natural beauty and the diversity of the homeland and in its verses to conjure up the mentality and describe the habits of the poet's people. As an authentic and harmonious work of art, integral in its conception, with a fine rhythm and with its powerful sound patterns, the poem is simultaneously both poetically gentle, resolute and solemn. Powerful and suggestive in its recitation, since its first publication the poem has had a huge public. In 1846 the young cadet of the 10th border infantry regiment Josip Runjanin composed the music to accompany its verse. At the beginning of the 1860s the poem was harmonized for a men's choir and it became exceptionally popular. During the competition held at the large exhibition of the Croatian-Slavonian Economic Society in Zagreb in 1891,under the title "Our Beautiful Homeland" the poem was proclaimed by a large majority the Croatian national anthem. Exactly a hundred years later, in the year when the Croatian state gained independence, it finally became the official national anthem.

Why this account of the anthem in the introduction to this kind of text? We mention the anthem because within the context of the time when it was written it expressed in succinct form, better than any other literary artifact, the essence of the Croatian land, its people and its history. It needs to be said that not many European nations possess a solemn song which, without battle cries or the flatulent rhetoric referring to ruler and state, with such sincere exultation celebrates the beauty and the diversity of the homeland, gently addresses it as "dear" and with an emphatic love speaks of the zeal and the habits of its people. Amongst the people "Our Beautiful Land" has become so popular that in everyday conversation it has become a synonym for Croatia itself.

That Croatia is truly a country of exceptional natural beauty, possessing a rich heritage, can be established by anyone who has attempted to know it in the abundance of its exceptional diversity. This includes its rich geographical morphology, the lushness, variety and the many specific rarities of its vegetation and animal life, the monuments of human habitation stretching from the earliest periods up to contemporary

times, its cities and settlements whose spatial layouts, functionality, buildings, monuments and pleasure gardens harmoniously fit into the Middle European, Pannonian and Mediterranean space.

The area of the contemporary Croatian state is relatively small – just over 56.000 square kilometers. However, this space in relation to its size is very convoluted and has the shape of a horseshoe whose northeastern tip encompasses the rim areas and parts of the Pannonian lowlands while its southern, longer but narrower part lies in the richly indented eastern coast of the Adriatic sea with its series of islands of which, if one includes the smallest, there are more than a thou-

Left: Velebit, Anića kuk

Right: Island of Korčula, morning mist over Vela Luka

sand. The central, connecting part of the horseshoe is made up of the peri-Pannonian area, the mountain-hilly region, the foothills and the river valleys which run on towards the Adriatic cost into the extreme northwestern part of the Dinara mountain chain.

The borders of today's Croatia have been determined both by geographical and political factors. Historical circumstances which throughout the centuries were unfavorable to the Croatian people have determined their living space. On the other hand, the large rivers in the continental part of the country are natural spatial boundaries while the mountain chains in the south have always been an obstacle to movements towards continental spaces. The history of the Croatian people, who since the early Middle Ages with their gradually obtained state independence affiliated themselves with broader social and political systems always on the contact zone between the West and the East, was frequently the element that tipped the scale within the region which was of immense, at times even of decisive, importance for the space of Europe. Since the 11th century church schism when it affiliated itself with the Roman church Croatia permanently aligned itself with the European

Left: Plitvice lakes, river Crna rijeka

Right: Island of Biševo nearby Vis, Blue cave

Scene from the Šibenik Zagora (hinterland) region

cultural, religious and political West and this has been its main and fateful determinant up to the present. During the Tartar invasion but especially during the period of the devastating onslaught of Ottoman forces on Europe, Croatia in the literal sense of the phrase became *antemurale christianitatis* (bulwark of Christianity) and almost bled to death defending Europe, while Europe itself, in most part preoccupied with dynastic disputes and military campaigns to conquer the enormous trans-oceanic spaces, almost peacefully found satisfaction in the achievements of Renaissance and Baroque art. But even during these four horrific centuries when it was divided amongst the Middle European powers of the time, individuals found the strength in Croatia to build, paint, sculpt, write, compose and to undertake scientific research.

Left: The distant island of Palagruža on the open sea

Right: Pelješac olive tree

Due to its spatial and historical position on the edge of the culture to which it belonged, a specific culture developed in Croatia in which some of the traits of earlier artistic styles

coexisted for a long time with new forms, merging with these new forms in wondrously ingenious and aesthetically most interesting works. Because of modest material possibilities, frequent devastations and renewals, Croatian material culture is not in most cases of large dimensions but it is great according to its spirit and the wondrous inspiration to create or to renew itself even in the most dire circumstances.

Life on the border, almost always under the threat of war, frequent migrations and the search for refuge, all of this shaped the specific mentality of the Croatian people who, although it somewhat varies in individual regions, show a series of common traits such as the simultaneous presence of both gentleness and decisiveness, hospitality and openness but primarily pride and devotion to one's people and tradition.

Croatia is a land shaped according to the measure of man. Its cities and settlements stand in a harmonious relationship with settled space. It has no formidably high mountains nor, excepting the border at the Danube, too broad rivers, neither moors nor the ungraspable plains while even the infinity of the sea can only be truly viewed only from the shores of the outer chain of islands or only partially from the shore of the sou-

Left: Pula, through the vaults of the amphitheatre

Below: Apses of Šibenik cathedral

Pula, the preserved southern chapel of the basilica of St. Mary of Formosa

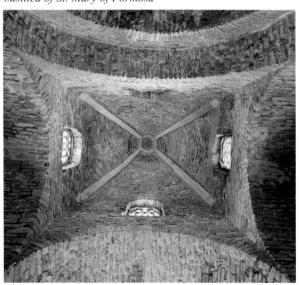

thern part of Croatia. Thusly, in spite of numerous contradictions and the wealth of its morphological diversity, the land of Croatia is a harmonious whole without pronounced extremes.

We recognize and differentiate four large geographical and, in large part, cultural wholes in Croatia. Adjoining its western and northern borders, central Croatia, through which pass the main river-ways, is the most densely populated area and in its middle stands the capital city Zagreb. Eastern Croatia is identical to the concept of Slavonia. Although it has mountains, valleys and hilly terrain it gains its basic characteristic from the flat plains of eastern Slavonia, Baranja and a part of western Srijem. Mountainous Croatia is formed by the last ranges of the Dinara mountains. It consists of two larger wholes – Gorski Kotar and Lika. This is the least populated area without a dominant urban center. The longest and the most indented, although because of the mountain massif a relatively narrow area, is littoral Croatia which according to natural morphology and the circumstances of historical development is divided into three wholes: Istria, Croatia's largest peninsula, Hrvatsko primorje (Croatian Littoral) whose land

Rosette on the Šibenik cathedral of St. Jacob

Right and below: Ring on the main portal of the Rector's palace

Below: Cathedral belfry viewed through the arches of the Peristyle

border is formed by the Velebit mountain chain while its sea border is formed by Kvarner bay with its islands. The southernmost Croatian province is Dalmatia which stretches out 400 kilometers in length from the last slopes of Velebit to the

11

Above: Dubrovnik, motif from the pleasure gardens on the island of Lokrum

Below: Motif from Kaštela

Right: Richly ornamented capitals of the outer portico of the Rector's palace

entrance into the bay of Boka Kotorska. The strings of larger and smaller islands in front of its cost are a constituent part of this whole.

MIDDLE CROATIA

In the geographical sense, central Croatia is a part of the southwestern rim of the peri-Pannonian space wherein morphologically coexist mountainous-hilly areas, foothills, riparian vallies and lowlands alongside larger rivers. The river Sava flows though this area, the longest and the largest river in Croatia. Its mountainous areas are of relatively low heights, covered with lush vegetation amongst which only the mountains Medvednica, Žumberačka gora and Ivančica rise over the height of a 1000 meters. The northern part is a particularly picturesque area which is gradually transformed into the valleys of the larger rivers Drava and Mura. The southern part is composed of the foothills and the plateaus alongside the rivers

Kupa, Korana, Mrežnica and Dobra.

Central Croatia, as the name indicates, is the core of the entire Croatian territory in which in a direct or an indirect manner all the components of the land of Croatia meet. It is the junction of all the more important horizontal, vertical and diagonal traffic routes through which throughout the centuries and even down the millenniums goods were exchanged and different cultures and habits interacted and permeated each other. The permanent strategic importance of this space caused its dense population and the rise of numerous cities, market places and strategically important fortifications. Today also the population of central Croatia is the highest amongst Croatian areas so that within the area covered by a third of Croatian territory almost a half of the entire population of Croatia (2.160.000 inhabitants) now lives. During the Middle Ages, almost in the spatial center at the juncture of various roads, a complex of neighboring settlements came into being which in time joined together and formed Zagreb, the capital of Croatia.

Zagreb - capital city of Croatia

Although the broader Zagreb area was inhabited as early as the prehistoric period (in Roman times the settlement Andautonia on the location of the present village Šćitarjevo) its real

Landscape of Hrvatsko Zagorje

Porch of the Croatian National Theatre

15

Left: Zagreb cathedral, above: the central nave

Below: Angel musician, detail of a fresco in the chapel of St. Stephen in the archbishop's palace (14th century)

Above: St. Dominic, St. Quirinus (?) and St. Francis, fresco in the sacristy of the Zagreb cathedral (13th century)

Below: God's Sepulcher, embroidery in relief, the treasury of Zagreb cathedral

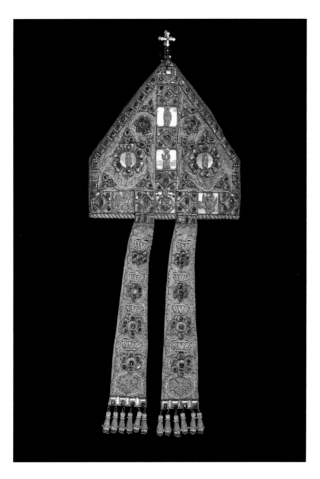

Left and above: Treasury of the Zagreb cathedral, bishop's miter 14th-16th century.

Right and above: Zagreb, the treasury of the cathedral, the miniature of Juraj de Topusko's missal, 15th-16th century

Right: Zagreb, Upper City, the parish church of St. Mark

Left: Zagreb, Stone gates

development began in the 11th century. Zagreb developed on the contact zone between the foothills of Medvednica mountain and the wide valley of the river Sava. In 1094 the Hungarian king Ladislav founded the Zagreb bishopric which proves that at that time the area was already densely populated. With the founding of the bishopric a "bishop's city" arose which consisted of the cathedral and the bishop's residence which were encircled by a common wall. The city expanded to the north with the addition of clergy's manors and with buildings belonging to other inhabitants encompassing the urban space called the Kaptol (capitulum) which was also fortified with walls. To the east an outskirt settlement inhabited by craftsmen and merchants who had arrived from regions where the Romance languages were spoken, probably from France and Belgium, grew which was called Laška, later Vlaška ves. On the neighboring hill, to the west of

Left and above:
Zagreb, the Baroque Oršić-Rauch palace, today the Croatian Historical Museum

Zagreb, Croatian Historical Museum, Vjekoslav Karas, Roman girl with lute (1845-1847)

Left and below: Zagreb, the Golden Hall of the one-time Department for Religious Affairs and Education

Above left: Golden hall, C. Medović, Arrival of the Croats

Above right: Golden hall, C. Medović, Church Council in Split

Right: Zagreb, the garden of the Meštrović atelier in Mletačka street

Below: From the Museum of the city of Zagreb

Above: Zagreb, fountain and the concert pavilion on Nikola Šubić Zrinski square

Right: Egyptological collection of the Archeological museum in Zagreb

Left: Zagreb, scenes from Ban Jelačić square

the Kaptol a typical merchant-craftsman settlement, called Gradec, developed. When the Hungarian king Bela IV found sanctuary here fleeing the Tatars, he gave the city by way of the Golden Bull the status of a free royal city which made it imperative that in a short time it be fortified by walls. Some of the dominant fortification points of the defense such as towers and fortified doors have been preserved up to the present day. In the valley between the hills not far from Manduševac spring a market space was formed while settlements grew around Gradec all the way to the rivulet Črnomerec to the west. Migration of population, particularly during the Turkish invasions in the 15th and the 16th century contributed to an intensification of settlement of both neighboring cities, their growth and the formation of new outskirts. The struggle for supremacy between the royal free city, which was already inhabited by a significant number of prominent noble families, and the fortified church center became very intensive so that the tensions frequently developed into open armed conflicts. The worldly power of Civil Croatia concentrated itself more and more in Gradec while the power of the Zagreb bishops made Kaptol the Croatian continental

Zagreb, the palace of the Croatian Academy of Science and Arts

Zagreb, the interior of the palace of the Croatian Academy of Science and Arts

church center. During the intensified danger from the Turks in the 16th century, Renaissance fortifications were erected around the cathedral and the bishop's residence and these in large part are still standing today. Since a significant part of the houses in Gradec and in the outskirts of the Kaptol were in large part built from wood frequent fires devastated different parts of the city. During the Baroque period, intensive construction of brick palaces in Gradec got under way, especially of noble palaces, public institutions, churches and monasteries (church of St. Catherine, Jesuit college, the convent of the Order of St. Clare, the Vojković-Oršić-Rauch palace, the Kulmer palace and many others). A large part of the old city of Zagreb, as is the case with the majority of Middle European cities, is characterized by the Baroque and later by a specific Middle European Biedermeier style, a more modest variant of Classicist monumentalism. The Kaptol during this period underwent expansion and intensive construction especially of a series of canonical residences, valuable architectonic works of the period. In 1669 the Jesuits in Zagreb founded an accredited University (restored in 1874 as the Royal university). By the emperor's decree in 1850 all the settlements and the old jurisdictions (Gradec, the Bishopric and the Kaptol) were unified into a single urban space – the free

Zagreb, Strossmayer's Gallery, Matteo da Milano, miniature from Alfonso d'Este's breviary (16th century)

Zagreb, Strossmayer's Gallery of Old Masters, Fra Angelico, Stigmatization of St. Francis

Right: Zagreb, F. Benković, "Abraham's Sacrifice" (around 1716), Strossmayer's Gallery of old masters

Below: Albrecht Dürer, Saint Ann with Mary and Jesus

Left:
Zagreb, Strossmayer's Gallery of Old Masters,
Antoine-Jean Gros, Madame Récamier (1825)

royal city of Zagreb. In such a manner the urban structure was integrated and the city descended from the hills onto the lowlands around the Sava river. This is the period during which the so-called Lower City was formed. The construction of the railroad line Sisak-Zagreb-Zidani Most in 1862, which connected the Croatian capital with Vienna and with Middle Europe, gave a special impetus to this urban growth. At this point the Western railway station was built while in 1890/91 the main railroad station was built on a flat area in the very midst of the newly built city. The railroad in large part determined the parameters of the new, contemporary city of Zagreb of the time. In 1880 Zagreb was hit by a devastating earthquake which brought about destruction and great damage but it at the same time stimulated reconstruction and an intensive buildup of a modern Middle European city. The enormous construction tasks of the time, particularly the rebuilding of the almost wholly destroyed cathedral demanded highly qualified architects. The central role in the enormous architectonic and urban endeavors was played by the architect and conservator Herman Bollé who was of German descent. Alongside the erection and reconstruction of

Above: Zagreb, Art pavilion

Right: Zagreb, Modern Gallery, V. Karas, Portraits of the married couple Krešić

Left: Zagreb, Modern Gallery, V. Bukovac, Patrician woman

Zagreb, Strossmayer square

Zagreb, V. Bukovac, "Gundulić's Dream", Modern gallery (1894)

Below: Zagreb, Klement Menci Crnčić, Still Sea; Modern Gallery

numerous buildings in Zagreb and other places in Croatia, special attention should be drawn to his reconstruction of the Zagreb cathedral in the neo-Gothic style and the large complex of arcades with cupolas, the church and other buildings in the central city cemetery Mirogoj. For the most part the Lower city of Zagreb was built in the then prevalent historicist architectural mode while from the end of the 19th century Art Nouveau buildings began to be dominant. The most significant and the most esteemed urban planning for the then contemporary Zagreb was carried out by the town planner Milan Lenuci who with his project of a series of mutually connected squares with a number of pleasure gardens and a great many green surfaces created the dominating space of the Lower City in the shape of a large horseshoe. In an exceptionally impressive manner this shape brings together, within a large space, the most important buildings of Croatian culture and science: the building of the head of the university, the Croatian national theatre, a number of important

Above: Zagreb, Modern Galley

Left: Zagreb, Modern Gallery, M. Rački, Francesca da Rimini

museums, the building of the Theatre Academy, buildings of the university, the brilliant Art Nouveau building of the University and the National Library (nowadays the Croatian State Archive), the Botanical gardens, the horticulturally well-designed Square of king Tomislav with the Art Pavilion, the square of Juraj Strossmayer with the palace of the Croatian Academy of Sciences and Art and with the Chemistry Institute and, finally, the square of Nikola Šubić Zrinski which has been designed as large gardens with high plane-trees, a fountain, a music pavilion and a series of sculpted busts of famous Croats. In such a manner the center of Zagreb was urbanistically ennobled and protected from the standard utilitarian construction as was abundant in European architecture during the 19th century. Between the two world wars Zagreb was built and it grew in the east-west direction on whose rims a large industrial zone came into being. After WWII the development of the city continued southward toward the river Sava. During the middle of the fifties, with the building of the Zagreb fair complex and a series of apartment blocks, the city of Zagreb crossed to the other shore of the Sava river and spread out onto the lowlands, particularly in the direction of Sisak. At the end of the twentieth century the growth of the city was paced down and replaced by a ring of satellite cities and settlements which now form the Zagreb urban region (Samobor, Zaprešić, Dugo Selo, Velika

Above: Zagreb, the façade of the Main Railway Station

Left: Zagreb, Robert Frangeš Mihanović, sculpture of king Tomislav

Right: Zagreb, the façade of the Croatian National Theatre, the work of the Wien architects Fellner and Helmer built in 1895.

Below: Zagreb, Starčević square

Vlado Bukovac, Croatian National Revival, ceremonious curtain of the Croatian National Theatre in Zagreb (1895)

Details of the interior of the auditorium of the Croatian National Theatre

Zagreb, Mimara Museum

Left: The vice-chancellor's building of Zagreb University

Below: Zagreb, I. Meštrović, History of the Croats

Gorica and others). Today the city of Zagreb has a bit over 700.000 inhabitants while with its urban region it is near to one million which is a little below one fourth of the entire population of Croatia. The main railroad junction, the crossroads of modern highways going north, west, south and east, with large and modern businesses, markets, banking and with the seats of

Above: Zagreb, the building of the Croatian state archive, formerly the University and National Library (arhitect Lubynski)

Right: Zagreb, the façade of the palace of the Croatian national bank

Below: Zagreb, I. Meštrović, exhibition pavilion of the Croatian Society of Visual Artists

Left: Façade of the Jesuit church in Zagreb

Zagorje landscape

Right: Veliki Tabor, cylinder-like tower and a part of the fortress

Left: Zagreb, Mirogoj cemetery, the church of Christ the King

central state institutions of government and administration, Zagreb is undoubtedly the dominant urban center of Croatia. With a University that integrates 33 faculties and academies, numerous institutes, over twenty museums and galleries of national significance, with its six theatres, concert halls, large number of publishing houses, libraries, cultural centers and the headquarters of numerous scientific, cultural and artistic associations, Zagreb is doubtlessly the spiritual center not only of Croatia but for all Croats.

To the northwest of the broader area of the city of Zagreb is Hrvatsko Zagorje one of the most picturesque regions within continental Croatia. The hills of Medvednica divide it from the city of Zagreb and this is the root of its name (zagorje in Croatian would mean tramontane region).

Hrvatsko Zagorje

The natural features of Hrvatsko Zagorje are hilly areas, crisscrossed by rivers and streams in whose middle rises a mountain chain known by the folk as Strahinčica while the Ivanščica hills cover the larger part of the central area of Zagorje. The height of this natural rock going through the middle of

Krapina, Hušnjakovo. Reconstruction of early humans in a half-cave that was inhabited by Neanderthal man (Krapina early humans)

Zagorje (Strahinčica 846 m, Ivanščica 1061 m) divides the space into two separate wholes – the southern part which by its location logically gravitates towards Zagreb and its broader area and the northern part which is oriented towards Varaždin as the most important economic and cultural center of northern Croatia. Alongside an abundance of water, Zagorje is characterized by a significant number of thermal and other medicinal springs which, accompanied by numerous natural beautiful spots and an exceptional rich cultural heritage, contributes to the tourist value of the region.

The presence of man in this area has continued almost since the dawn of humankind. In 1899, not far from Krapina on Hušnjakovo hill, the famous Croatian palaeontologist Dragutin Gorjanović-Kramberger discovered a large site with the remains of Neanderthal man. The bones and the stone artifacts of the diluvial man, more than 50.000 years old, were found in his original abode in the depth of a cave and are one of the most significant findings of the ancient human forefather on European soil. In the vicinity of the finding the life of early man is picturesquely ren-

dered with a series of bronze human figures and animals in natural sizes while in the near future the building of a very modern museum will be completed on the very location of this important finding. Findings from later periods, particularly from Roman times, evince that a developed civilization existed within this area. The Middle Ages, particularly from the beginning of the 12th century, are represented by fortified feudal cities – burghs located on elevated places or on the slopes of hills. Sad to say many have been deserted for a long time and today are no more than ruins, while some of them were renovated at a later date, particularly at the end of the 19th century, when they were given more luxuriant form in the spirit of historicist neo-stylistic ideas.

Sheltered by the Maceljsko, Varaždinskotopličko and Kalničko string of hills and by Medvednica mountain to the south, throughout history Hrvatsko Zagorje was a territory which was not immediately exposed to enemy onslaughts which for the greater part came from the east-west direction by way of the main traffic routes which went through the lowlands and the flows of the large rivers. In such a manner it was protected from

Above: The fortified squirearchical burgh Veliki Tabor nearby Desnići.

Below: Zagorje motif

On the next pages:
Hrvatsko Zagorje

large scale destruction and during the long turbulent centuries of constant threats, especially from the time of the first fierce incursions of the Turks to the west, it served as a relatively safe haven for numerous movements of people fleeing the conquerors from the east. A consequence of such centuries-old massive settling of people is the high density of population in the region, the highest in Croatia. In time the land holdings became so small that these became an obstacle to the survival of a population which made its livelihood from agriculture. This is the reason why

Kumrovec, ethno-village

during the last decades of the 19th century Zagorje became a region of emigrants. The drain of a part of the population to the south into Zagreb which at the time became an important industrial center and to the north into Varaždin which had become the regional center could not absorb the entire influx of the working force. This accounts for the fact that a numerous segment of Croatia's economic emigration abroad originated in Zagorje. Along with the fleeing common folk numerous noble families settled in the Zagorje area who, during the Baroque period and during the 19th century, built on their land holdings, according to their material resources, numerous noble residences but spacious castles as well or, coming into the possession of a holding,

Klanjec, Gallery of the sculptor Antun Augustinčić

Oršić castle in Gornja Stubica, today the Museum of the Peasant rebellion

Gubec's lime-tree in Donja Stubica

restored old Medieval burghs. Smaller city centers rose either at the outskirts of burghs or as markets at the crossroads alongside rivers. Rural settlements were located on the hillsides, frequently by joining together a number of villages or by connecting villages alongside the roads. The density of the population was the reason for the construction of a large number of sacral buildings of which one can, as a specific type, isolate parish fęte churches surrounded by a cinktor - a fenced space around a church - with its wall which on the inner side has a vaulted portico. Thusly on the occasion of patron-saint's days these churches could accommodate within their walls a significant number of people. In the Zagorje region the Paulist order made a significant contribution to religious art, not only by founding one of its most important monasteries in Lepoglava but also by the fact that the Paulist painted and decorated many other, especially parish fête churches.

According to the concentration of preserved monuments of culture Hrvatsko Zagorje can be numbered amongst the richest cultural areas in Croatia. The length of this text does not allow a broader listing but, heeding extreme reduction, one has to mention the burghs of Belecgrad, Loborgrad, and Trakošćan which

Antun Augustinčić, monument commemorating the Peasant Rebellion and Matija Gubec in Gornja Stubica, 1973

Belec, the parish church of St. Mary of the Snows, the interior

the famous Drašković counts in the 19th century restored as a luxuriant castle in the neo-Gothic style and surrounded it with gardens. In addition there is Veliki tabor not distant from Desinići which was built in the 12th century, the seat of the Celje counts, expanded in the 15th and the 16th century while its contemporary appearance dates from the first decades of the 19th century. This complex and multi-layered edifice belongs to monuments of the highest category.

Numerous castles of Croatian nobility families were built as permanent residences on their land holdings so that economic buildings were constructed next to them but gardens as well tended with an exceptional feeling for measure and taste. A part of these castles served as summer houses for relaxation and for social gatherings, especially for the hunt. If we take into account their representative quality, the high and demanding standards of decoration it can be said that only a number of similar residences of the Slavonian nobility can match them in the entire area of continental Croatia. Along with the already mentioned Trakošćan one has to remember Bežanec of the Keglević counts, Nove

Belec, the parish church of St. Mary of the Snows, part of the cinktor

Right: Lepoglava, Paulist monastery church of St. Mary, sanctuary. Fresco "Jesus Banishing Merchants from the Temple" by I. Ranger and the painted choir seats

Lepoglava, Paulist monastery church of St. Mary, façade

Lepoglava, Paulist monastery church of St. Mary, view of the choir

The Classicist parish church of Our Lady's Assumption in Pregrada, choir

Right: Krapina, the Franciscan church of St. Catherine, the main altar

dvore near Zaprešić which were in the possession of the Zrinski counts and which were finally in 1852 bought by the Croatian Vice-Roy Josip Jelačić. The Baroque castle Lužnica was the possession of the noble families Čikulin and Rauch. The most beautiful classicist castle Januševac was built around 1830 by general Vrkljan. Mention ought to be made of the castles Laduč, Miljana, Oršić, Jakovlje but this is only a small sampling of the wealth of buildings in Zagorje.

Of the sacral edifices one ought to mention the parish fête church of the Mother of God of the Snows in Belec which is marked by an exceptional wealth of Baroque altars and the illusionist paintings of the Paulist Ranger. The votive church of Saint Mary of

47

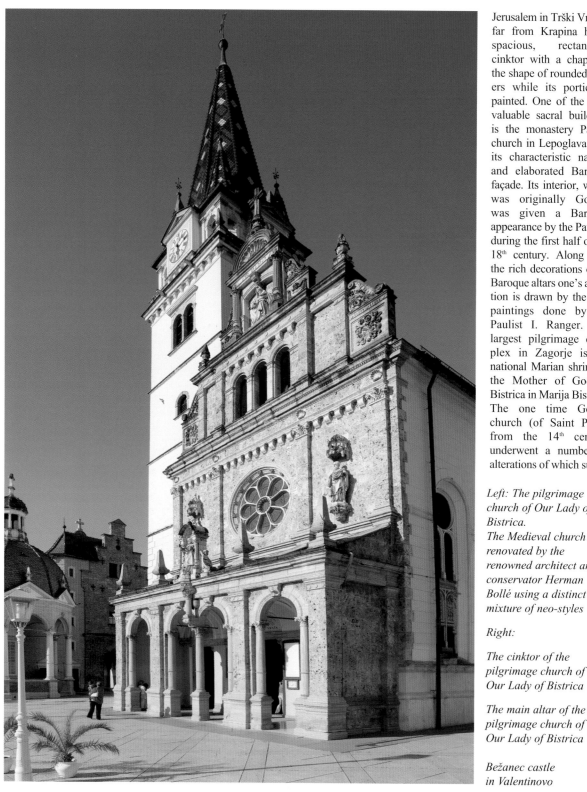

Jerusalem in Trški Vrh not far from Krapina has a spacious, rectangular cinktor with a chapel in the shape of rounded towers while its portico is painted. One of the most valuable sacral buildings is the monastery Paulist church in Lepoglava with its characteristic narrow and elaborated Baroque façade. Its interior, which was originally Gothic, was given a Baroque appearance by the Paulists during the first half of the 18th century. Along with the rich decorations of its Baroque altars one's attention is drawn by the wall paintings done by the Paulist I. Ranger. The largest pilgrimage complex in Zagorje is the national Marian shrine of the Mother of God of Bistrica in Marija Bistrica. The one time Gothic church (of Saint Peter) from the 14th century underwent a number of alterations of which surely

Left: The pilgrimage church of Our Lady of Bistrica.
The Medieval church was renovated by the renowned architect and conservator Herman Bollé using a distinct mixture of neo-styles

Right:

The cinktor of the pilgrimage church of Our Lady of Bistrica

The main altar of the pilgrimage church of Our Lady of Bistrica

Bežanec castle in Valentinovo

49

On previous pages: Trakošćan, the castle of the Drašković counts   *Trakošćan, the castle of the Drašković counts, interiors*

the most consequential were those done at the beginning of the 1880s by the architect and conservator H. Bollé in the historicist spirit and meshing together elements of the Gothic, the Baroque and the Florence and German Renaissance.

Of the museums mention ought to be made of the Museum of the Peasant Rebellion in Gornja Stubica, the ethno-village in Kumrovac and the commemorative collection of the famous Croatian sculptor Antun Augustinčić in Klanjec.

The most important settlements in Hrvatsko Zagorje are Krapina (the center of the county), Parešić which falls into the orbit of the broader Zagreb area and Ivanec to the north.

Today the thermal springs are organized not only as health locations but as very attractive tourist and recreational destinations. Of these the better known are the Stubički, Krapinski, Tuheljski and Varaždinski spas.

The northern part of Hrvatsko Zagorje, Međimurje and upper Podravina, are areas which naturally gravitate towards the largest city center of this part of Croatia, the city of Varaždin. Since the city of Čakovec, the largest settlement and administrative center of Međimurje county, is barely 14 kilometers distant from Varaždin, it can be concluded that these two cities, although divided by the river Drava, with their almost integrated economic area, form the central urban core towards which gravitate all the surrounding areas.

Varaždin

The city of Varaždin was first mentioned in 1181 in a document by the Hungarian-Croatian king Bele III. In this document it is mentioned as the royal fortress Garestin. Without doubt this was a larger army camp over which presided representatives of royal authority. Beneath the fortress a city settlement of craftsmen and merchants developed, Varaždin, on which the Hungarian-Croatian king Andrew II in his 1202 charter bestowed the status of a free royal city. In such a manner these two separate urban entities existed in a manner of mutual dependence until in 1850 the Austrian administration unified them. During the Turkish threat and especially after the 16th century, Varaždin played an exceptional role in the defense of Croatian territory and became the most important fortress of the Slavonian military region. During the 17th and the 18th century, by redoing older buildings in the Baroque mode and with the construction of new sacral edifices, palaces for the nobility and public buildings, it acquired the appearance of a typical Medieval Baroque city. Varaždin was the seat

Right:
Varaždin, the interior of the old city

Varaždin, the old city

Varaždin, the horticultural outlay of the city cemetery

Left and above: Varaždin, city town-hall

Left and below: Varaždin, the Sermage palace

of the Croatian Vice-Roy and the Croatian Royal council, that is, it was the political and administrative center of Croatia. The catastrophic fire which devastated the city in 1776 forced the Vice-Roy and the administration to again remove to Zagreb. Although almost three fourths of the houses were destroyed, Varaždin was rebuilt in no more than a few years. Today, with its 50 thousand dwellers, Varaždin is an exceptionally coherent urban environment in whose historical core Gothic, Baroque, Biedermeier and historicist buildings almost organically coexist giving it an appearance and the significance of one of the most beautiful and most valuable locations in continental Croatia. The Old City stands out with its Gothic base, the town hall, numerous Baroque palaces of famous Croatian noble families, numerous churches, the theatre and the extraordinary horticultural complex of Varaždin cemetery, unique in Croatia.

Varaždin is the center of the textile and food industry, a highway junction but primarily an important educational and cultural center whose importance transcends regional frameworks.

Twenty kilometers southeast of the city lie the Varždinski spas, today an important health and tourist center with a great tradition. During Roman times the famous healing thermae Aquae Iasae were built here whose rich archeological remains bear witness to the distinctly high quality of antique buildings and its sculpting skills.

Međimurje

Međimurje, the area between the rivers Drava and Mura, is the northernmost as well as the smallest Croatian district. The hilly area was predestined for intensive farming, particularly for vineyards and fruit growing on the Međimurje hill fields. Wooded expanses have been preserved in the river Mura lowland which are an almost untouched ecological complex which has been made into a natural preserve. The city of Čakovec is the center of Međimurje. In the 13th century here stood a powerful fortress while in the 15th century a craftsmen-merchant settlement rose alongside the fortress. In 1546 Čakovec became the seat of the most powerful Croatian noble

Above: Čakovec, fortress

Below: Art Nouveau house in Čakovec

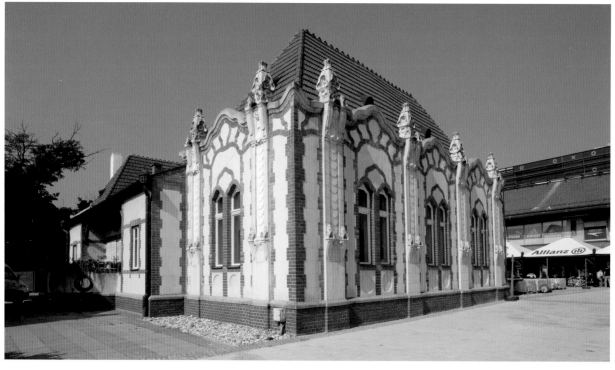

family, the Zrinski counts and it remained so up to the tragic year 1671 when, after the Zrinsko-Frankopani plot against the Vienna court, this famous noble branch and the hope of Croatia of the time was almost uprooted and all of its possessions requisitioned and acquired by the emperor. The Zrinski family built in Čakovec the so-called Old castle, in reality a mighty fortress, and the New castle, a residential Baroque palace. The flatland city of Čakovec is a well-ordered and polished urban center which is dominated by relatively low buildings. The complex of buildings in the city center built in the shape and with the decoration of the Hunagarian Art Nouveau movement are of special interest.

Podravina

To the east, south of the river Drava lies Podravina. This area is not a compact whole because due to a number of geographical and historical circumstances parts of Podravina gravitate to different centers. Upper Podravina between the river Drava and the Zagorje hills, according to its spatial logic, gravitate to Varaždin and its region. Middle Podravina, between the river Drava and Bilogora is a separate whole with a number of smaller gravitational centers, while lower Podravina between the river Drava and the Papučko-Krndijsko gorje hills gravitate towards Osijek, that is to eastern Croatia. Thusly the first two areas are a part of Middle Croatia while the latter belong to eastern Croatia.

Upper Podravina lacks any prominent urban center precisely because of its close connection to Varaždin and partially to Koprivnica. The most important settlement within this area is Ludbreg so that frequently this area, bordered by the lower flow of the river Bednja, is called Ludgreška Podravina.

Middle Podravina is situated between the river Drava and the wooded high grounds of Bilogora to the south. The attraction of the inundatory areas alongside the Drava river are the settlements which have changed their position, whose inhabitants moved to areas which were not endangered by floods. Through the millenniums the river Drava deposited large quantities of sand in layers as high as 80 meters so that the once well-known Đurđevački peski sands were a real sand desert across which the winds created dunes. Today this has been stabilized by a layer of vegetation.

Koprivnica

The largest center of this region is the city of Koprivnica whose roots are known to be in the 13th century while as early as 1356 the city had the status of a free royal city. Koprivnica is located on an almost ideal site where Podravina adjoins Posavina so that with the construction of the railroad line Budapest-Zagreb (1870), and the later extension of this line to Rijeka and the building of the railroad line Zagreb-

Koprivnica

Đurđevac, fortified city (14th-16th century)

Koprivnica-Osijek it gained in importance as a significant transportation junction. With the construction of the later Podravina highway its importance only grew. Parallel to the transportation system, the economic function of the city also grew so that Koprivnica is the seat of the largest and the most successful Croatian complex of the food industry, the famous "Podravka" plant which stimulates the most diverse agricultural activity in the broader area.

Đurđevac

All of the more important settlements of middle Podravina are located along the highway and railroad line in the direction of Osijek, the capital city of Slavonia. Of the more important settlements one must mention Đurđevac about which there are written sources dating to as early as the 13th century. In the 14th century a well fortified burgh was built which became the center of defense during the Ottoman invasion. In 1552 Đurđevac withstood a Turkish siege about which a witty legend was concocted concerning hens shot from cannon against the Turkish encircling forces by which the defenders sought to convince the enemy that they still had abundant food supplies. During the period of the Croatian Military Border Đurđevac was a significant point of the defense and the seat of the border regiment.

Hlebine

Of the Podravina villages certainly the most famous is Hlebine, the "birthplace" of Croatian naive art. In 1929 the renowned Croatian painter Krsto Hegedušić initiated amongst the young talented Hlebine peasants a course in painting as one of the activities of the artistic group "Earth". Without any doubt amongst them the most talented was Ivan Generalić, the most famous name of Croatian and newer European naive art of the 20th century. Later a group of his most gifted followers created a specific mode of artistic expression painting on glass so that one can speak of the Hlebine school of Croatian naive art. The famous gallery of the works of Ivan Generalić and his artistic followers is located in Hlebine.

Virovitica

Virovitica is the easternmost city in Podravina. In the 13th century the Hungarian great lord confirmed its freedoms while from the same period we find mention of a Franciscan and a Dominican monastery. A mighty burgh encircled by water was built during the Middle Ages. The Turks lay siege to it for 130 years. At the beginning of the 19th century, on the same location on the ruins of the burgh, count Pejačević

Ivan Generalić, Woodcutter

erected a monumental Baroque-classicist castle surrounded by a park and a ditch. Today Virovitica is a city with large food industries amongst which the dominant one is the very modern sugar factory.

The Bjelovar region

In defining the eastern part of middle Croatia we descend into the space south of Podravina which is a kind of geographical link between the rivers Sava and Drava. In the broader sense we can call this the Bjelovar region although the city itself is not such a powerful gravitational center capable of integrating the entire area. A number of smaller centers to which gravitate parts of the area divide the entire space into a number of counties: Bjelovar-Bilogora, Koprivnica-Križevci, partially Virovitica-Podravina, Slavonia-Požega, Sisak-Moslavina and even Zagreb county.

The geographic morphology of this area consists of the Lonjsko-ilovska zavala basin, a gently rolling area through which flow the rivers Česma, Ilova and Pakra while the area itself is bounded by the eastern part of Medvednica mountain to the west, the Kalničko gorje hills and the Bilogora high grounds to the north, the ridges of the Slavonian mountains of Papuk and Psunj to the east while to the south rises the lonesome Moslavačka gora mountains. Owing to the relatively late tectonic movements the fault line which was created in the foothills of the fringe Slavonian mountains brought to the surface thermal springs which for their medicinal quality were known as early as Antiquity. At the same time, to the southwest of the basin, south of Moslavačka gora mountains large quantities of oil and gas were discovered whose exploitation began in the 50ies of the 20th century.

Throughout the centuries the fate of the people of this region was determined by the fact that it was a decisive defe. e zone against the onslaught of Ottoman forces against the West. As a part of the Croatian Military Border, forever on the border where two civilizations and their armies met, this area for centuries experienced the insecurity of life on the border, continuous war and post-war migrations of population as well as the systematic, planned settlement by different peoples of the Austrian monarchy. This area has the largest number of national minorities in the whole of Croatia. Alongside a numerous Czech and Slovakian minority we find representatives of the Hungarian, Ukrainian, German and even Italian national group. When they settled here these people brought with them new knowledge and skills which advanced the agriculture and introduced previously unknown activities. Along with all the peculiarities of customs, the cultural wealth of different people is the true amalgam of this area.

Bjelovar

The largest city of the region is Bjelovar and it is relatively speaking a young city (18th century). It arose as a typical seat of the military administration and the quarters for the concentration of troops within this sector of the Croatian Military Border. Like all of the other cities belonging to the old Croatian Military Border the city of Bjelovar is an urban space with a regular screen of streets and with a spacious central square on which are located all the more important administrative and military buildings, the school and the parish church. After the abolishment of the Croatian Military Border it became the administrative center of the region but being outside the main traffic routes it did not succeed in imposing itself as a significant center outside of its more immediate region.

Križevci

Križevci is a very old city with a rich history. Since the 12th century it has been the center of a county. During the fierce dynastic struggle for the Hungarian-Croatian throne, the famous "bloody parliament" was held in Križevci in 1397 during which followers of king Žigmund murdered a number of prominent Croatian noblemen. In the 19th century Križevci found itself on the railroad line Zagreb-Budapest and this had a favorable influence on its economic development. Križevci is the seat of the Croatian Greek-Catholic bishopric. Since the Križevci region, especially the Kalnik foothills, is an area rich in vineyards here we find the so-called Križevci statutes, a listing of rules which prescribed the behavior of the members of the association of drinkers of good wine during "wine rituals". Since the 17th century the customs of the "statutes" were spread by word of mouth but later they were published in a number of variants. In the beginning "the rituals of drinking wine" were organized in the residences of the nobility while from the 19th century they were accepted by the city folk.

Daruvar

Daruvar is a city with a long spa health tradition dating back to Antiquity. It rose on the land holdings of count Janković who built bath buildings along his Baroque castle. Today Daruvar is the center of the Czech minority in Croatia.

Pakrac

Pakrac stands on the western foothill of Psunj. In the 13th century it was the seat of the Templers while during the Turkish occupation it was an administrative center. After the liberation from the Ottomans, Italians settled in the Pakrac

Left: Križevci, Greek Catholic cathedral

region and they have managed to preserve their language and customs to the present. Not far from Pakrac is Lipik, a well known and luxuriously constructed thermal spa with a French type park.

The area alongside the river Lonja

To the south of Podravina, north of the river Sava, lies the large inundatory field Lonjsko polje. For a part of its course the river Lonja flows parallel to the river Sava. In order to regulate this often flooded area a 105 kilometers long canal Lonja-Strug was constructed. In this area which stretches between Ivanić Grad, Kutina and Novska there are significant findings of oil and natural gas. As an ornithological preserve, a part of Lonja field has been protected as a natural park. Baroque wooden chapels and traditional houses made out of wood have been preserved in this Posavina area.

Turopolje

The river Odra flows south from the river Sava. Between Odra and the low Vukomeričke gorice hills spreads out the area of Turopolje. Historically speaking, this area is interesting because of the specific circumstances in which Hungarian kings gave the status of royal officials and noblemen to some Turoplje families whose members were in the service as officials in the castle in Zagreb. On the basis of this, numerous branches of heirs of these families appropriated the right of some kind of village nobility out of which developed the autonomous status of "the noble county of Turopolje". In the struggles with powerful feudal families many rulers confirmed the autonomy of the Turoplje people which was eventually abolished by the French when they administered the so-called Illyrian provinces during the rule of Napoleon I. On the northwestern rim of Turopolje stands Velika Gorica, a city with about 40.000 inhabitants which today belongs to the ring of satellite cities encircling Zagreb.

Banovina

The area south of the Sava river, marked by the rivers Glina and Kupa, to the south by Zrinska gora hills and to the east by the river Una which is the Croatian boundary with Bosnia and Herzegovina, is called Banovina. During the period of the Croatian Military Border this was the Vice-Roy's March and it was directly under the command of the Croatian Vice-Roy. The Posavina part of Banovina is low while to the south it becomes hilly and afterwards mountainous, gradually rising to Zrinska gora hills which are over 600 meters high. Throughout its history, this part of Croatia has been affected by constant enemy threats, frequent migrations of the population and military rule over the area. The area is sparsely populated and the urban centers in large part carry the seal of typical urban centers in which military authority was in power.

Sisak, the old city

Sisak

The largest urban center of Banovina is Sisak, a very old city. The one time Celtic Segestica was subdued by Roman troops who built their own city Siscio. The Roman city was destroyed in the 6th century during the Avars-Slav onslaught. According to Carolingian sources, during the 8th century it was the fortress of the Pannonian-Croatian duke Ljudevit of Posavina. During the fierce Turkish attacks in the 16th century Sisak had a particular strategic significance. Because of this the Zagreb Kaptol at the very place where the river Kupa merges with the river Sava built a powerful fortress with a triangular ground plan and with three cylindrical towers at the angles. In 1593 a fateful battle took place under the city of Sisak in which the forces of the Vice-Roy defeated the many times more numerous Turkish army. This significant victory put a stop to the further onslaught of the Ottomans towards Zagreb and the remaining free parts of Croatia. The old city of Sisak (the market and the craftsmen quarters) and New Sisak (the military quarters) joined together to form a unified free royal city only in 1871. After WWII heavy industry, a large ironworks, an oil refinery and other plants were built in Sisak which in time lost their original significance particularly after the heavy devastation they underwent during the Homeland war. The construction of a modern highway connecting Sisak to Zagreb and the restoration of the harbor on the river Sava will doubtlessly restore the importance of this city.

Petrinja

Petrinja is only twenty kilometers distant from Sisak so that in reality it is its double settlement. In history it played a significant role in the defense against the Ottoman onslaught while during the last century of the existence of the Croatian Military Border it was the main military seat of the Vice-Roy's March. Today Petrinja is an economically significant center with an important industry of meat processing. Of the smaller towns mention must be made of Glina, an important military center during the time of the Croatian Military Border and Topusko where health tourism has developed because of the thermal springs.

Public gardens in the center of Glina

Fašnik (carnival) in Samobor

The Žumberak region

Žumberak, the highest mountainous area of middle Croatia, represents the southwestern part of the broader Zagreb region. Žumberak mountains which are 1178 meters high and the somewhat lower Samobor hills are a space where are located a number of smaller settlements built at the height of 500 and even up to 700 meters. The population of Žumberak consists of an autochthonous Croatian populace and Vlach settlers who came to these parts serving in the army of the Croatian Military Border. In the 17th century these Orthodox believers began to convert to the Greek-Catholic religion so that the entire Žumberak area along with the Križevci area are the only areas in Croatia settled by Greek-Catholics.

Samobor

Samobor is the largest city settlement of the broader Žumberak area. The old Samobor burgh was built in the 13th century while it obtained the status of a free royal city at the same time as Zagreb. Samobor is a picturesque town which in its center has preserved its original, in large part, Baroque core. Having become a satellite city within the Zagreb belt, modern Samobor has grown into an attractive place of residence while its picturesque surroundings are the basis of its excursion tourism. The commercial zone of Samobor and the nearby Sveta Nedelja have today become an exemplary case of successful investments in effective smaller plants.

Jastrebarsko

On the road to Karlovac, some thirty kilometers from Zagreb stands Jastrebarsko, the center of the Plešivica foothills. Surrounded by vineyards it is the center of the wine-growing industry of the foothill area. A castle with four wings and two powerful round towers at its angles was built in Jastrebarsko in the 16th century. It belonged to the famous Eddödy noble family. The portico with arcades inside the court-yard dates from the previous Baroque building.

Karlovac and the Kordun region

Karlovac, the largest city amongst those which surround the Croatian metropolis, is located some fifty kilometers to the southwest of Zagreb. It is a relatively recently founded city. It was established in 1579 out of the dire need to directly protect Austrian imperial territory which in this area was no more than fifty kilometers separated from the Turkish military border. Karlovac was built on the initiative of the archduke Charles Hapsburg after whom it got its name. The city was built according to the contemporary fortification programs of the late Renaissance as a power-

Karlovac, the early Baroque Franciscan and parish church of the Most Holy Trinity on the main square

ful fort shaped like a six-forked star which at that time enabled a simultaneous defense from all sides with cannon support from the large pentagon bastions. Karlovac was founded on a strategically ideal place, on the junction where four rivers meet: Kupa, Korana, Mrežnica and the Dobra river. The fact that it was surrounded by water enhanced its defensive capabilities. Its urban core was subordinated to its defensive function. Conceptualized as an ideal city, the city in the middle of the fortification had an orthogonal grill of streets and a central rectangular square. The building of the city fortifications lasted almost two hundred years and the task was impeded by frequent flooding. Gradually it lost its important strategic role especially after the peace treaty in Srijemski Karlovci. Up to 1777 it was under the jurisdiction of the Croatian Military Border but that year it received the status of a free royal city. Located in a place which ideally connected the roads going in the direction north-south towards the Austrian Adriatic harbors and relying on the navigability of the river Kupa up to its merging with the Sava river, in the 19th century Karlovac quickly developed as a market and a craft center. The building of the railroad from Zagreb to Rijeka in 1873 fundamentally disrupted its market function so that a process of restructuration took place that turned the city to industry. This trend continued between the two world wars

Above: Ozalj, entrance gate into the fortified city

Below: The fortified city Ribnik nearby Ozalj, 13th-14th century

and after WWII large scale and modern industrialization set in. In the most recent times Karlovac is undergoing a new process of restructuration especially after the completion of the building of modern highways in the direction of Split and Rijeka. Today Karlovac has almost merged with the twenty kilometers distant town of Duga Resa, once a strong center of the textile industry and today a zone of modern handicraft plants and service industries.

To the south of Karlovac lies the picturesque hilly area of Kordun, once an important defense area of the Croatian Military Border. Next to Slunj stands the village Rastoke where the river Slunjčica branches out into a number of backwaters. Over gypsum barriers and falls it flows into the Korana. Since people used the abundance of quick-flowing falls in the past there were many

Rastoke nearby Slunj

mills on the river (up to 60). Today there are only a few and they are protected as cultural monuments.

EASTERN CROATIA

Eastern Croatia consists of Slavonia, the southern Croatian part of Baranja and western Srijem. The lowland part of Slavonia is adjoined in the north to the river Drava and in the south to Slavonian Posavina. Požega valley, surrounded by the mountain ranges of Psunj, Papuk, Krndija, Dilj and Požeška gora, is located in its central part.

Slavonija

Slavonian Podravina encompasses the northwestern part of eastern Croatia located between the river Drava and the slopes of the mountain massif of the western Slavonian hills. An inundatory plain stretches out along the Drava river and is for the most part covered with forests while the more southern parts of this area are conjoined to the foothills of the mountains of Papuk and Krndija.

The Slavonia Podravina region

The main roads and the railroad lines run along the contact zone between the flatland and the foothills and this is where stand the larger settlements of Slatina, Orahovica and Našice. Large woody regions once covered a great part of Slavonia. The exploitation of high quality wood especially of the Slavonian oak began in the second half of the 19th century so that the extent of the wooded region is today greatly reduced. Forestry and the wood processing industry make up the greater part of the economy of this region. The largest settlement of this region is Slatina. Already in the 13th century it was mentioned as a fair and today it is a smaller industrial center. Našice stands on the very place where the foothills of Krndija merge with the lowland. In the 13th century the city was mentioned as the possession of the Templer order and the Aba family who built a burgh. Franciscans, whose parish church is the church of St. Anthony of Padua, are recorded on their property as early as the 13th century. A number of rulers came and went in this region up to the 16th century. The last ones before the Turkish occupation were the counts of Ilok. After the liberation from the Ottoman empire the buildings were given a Baroque look. In 1812 the famous duke family

Above: Našice, the castle of the Pejačević counts

Below: Našice, public gardens

Pejačević built in Našice a one-storey classicist castle in the middle of a large park arranged in the English manner. In 1909 the Pajčević family built another one-storey castle while during the 1880ies the famous architect Herman Bollë built a neo-Gothic chapel with a crypt for the noble family. The well-known Croatian composer Dora Pejačević created her work in Našice. Nearby Našice is Đurđenovac the center of the Slavonian wood processing industry.

The Papuk foothills gravitate towards Orahovica. Medieval sources indicate that it arose under Ružica-city, a complex of Medieval fortresses, amongst the largest in Croatia whose imposing ruins can even today be seen to the west, nearby Orahovica. The castle and the series of stone fortifications formed a unique complex whose walls were up to 9 meters thick. To the south, standing alone, is the Orthodox monastery of St. Nicholas

Above: Donji Miholjac, a park with exotic plants encircles Majláth castle

Left: Donji Miholjac, the castle of count Majláth, central "tower"

Right: Valpovo, the Hilleprand-Prandau-Normann castle, Gothic chapel

whose church was built in the tradition of the Moravian school. Of the natural sights mention should be made of the park-forest Jankovac.

Donji Miholjac stands along the Drava river on the once strategic crossing across the river. At the beginning of the 20th century count Majláth had a historicist castle, surrounded with a spacious park containing exotic vegetation, built on the once noble land holdings of the Prandau family.

Somewhat to the east lies Valpovo, in the Middle Ages a squirearchical land holding of a number of families. Documents pertaining to the existence of the Valpovo burgh date from the beginning of the 15th century. After the liberation of Slavonia from the Turks in the 18th century, the fortified city became the property of the Hilleprand-Prandau family which transformed it into a castle. At the end of the 19th century it became the property of the Normann family. A spacious landscape park surrounds the castle. Nearby Belišće is the center of the wood processing industry.

Above: Kutjevo, the Jesuit residence and the parish church of St. Mary

Below: Požega

The Požega valley

The Požega valley lies in the center of the western Slavonian hills. A ring of hills isolated this area from Slavonian Podravina and opened it up towards the south in the direction of Slavonian Posavina. The rivers Orljava and Londža flow along the rim of the valley and connect near Pleternica and as a single river flow into the Sava. Already in Roman times this area was renowned for its fertility so that it was called the Golden valley (Vallis aurea). In addition to cereals, vineyards developed from of old in the valley itself on its foothill rims. Today it produces some of the most esteemed

Kutjevo vineyards

Croatian wines. Not far from here are located the wine cellars of Kutjevo, the wine-industry center of the region.

Požega

The urban center of the valley is Požega whose burgh dates back to the 12th century. In the middle of a rich agricultural region, Požega very soon became the most important Slavonian city. Even during the Turkish occupation it was the administrative center of the greater part of Slavonia. After the retreat of the Turks the city was restored in Baroque forms and became one of the most important merchant, handicraft and, owing to the presence of the Jesuits, educational and cultural center. In the 19th century the urban structure was partially modified owing to the construction of Biedermeier and historicist edifices. At the beginning of the 20th century the city was enriched by buildings built in the spirit of the Art Nouveau movement. Owing to extended conservation enterprises today Požega is one of the most tidy and attractive continental Croatian cities.

The Slavonia Posavina region

A number of important settlements developed on the Slavonian part of Posavina which was once on the very border of the two empires and later on the main thoroughfare in the direction west-east.

Slavonski Brod

The largest of these is Slavonski Brod, today the regional center. Throughout its long history (Roman Marsonia) the city had an exceptionally important strategic position because of the fact that it was located on an ideal place where transversal thoroughfares intersected with those that led across the river into Serbia. It suffered heavy devastation a number of times so that numerous monuments from the Middle Ages were not preserved. In the 18th century a strong fortress was built in Brod, one of the largest on the border with the Ottoman empire. Military buildings are located within the square space of the fortress while the fortress

Slavonian flatlands

itself was defended by a whole complex of bastions and ditches. Today Slavonski Brod is an important industrial center to which gravitates the Posavian part of Slavonia. Vineyards successfully grow on the not distant slopes of mountain Dilj gora.

Nova Gradiška

Nova Gradiška lies to the west of Slavonski Brod, a city that grew out of a settlement dating to the Croatian Military Border. Gradiška connects Posavina with the Požega valley. Along the river Sava there is a series of settlements on the main transversal communication thoroughfare – Okučani, Vrpolje, Slavonski Šamac.

The entire area of eastern Croatia gravitates towards its main urban center – Osijek, so that this area can be called the Osijek macro-region.

Osijek

Osijek is located on a one time strategically important location – the crossing of the river Drava into Podunavlje and on the road from Hungary to Bosnia and the Adriatic. During

Osijek, Tvrđa, Kužni pil

Below: Osijek, Tvrđa, the Baroque church of St. Michael   *Above: Osijek, Tvrđa, city walls*

Roman times it began as a fortress on the border to afterwards become the city Mursa having the status of a colony. During the Middle Ages a citadel protected the crossing across the Drava. The Turks overran it in 1526 and held it under their control up to 1687. Turkish Osijek possessed oriental features with a number of mosques. During the period of Turkish rule the famous wooden bridge was built over the Drava and the nearby swamps all the way to the village Darda, almost 10 kilometers long. After the liberation from the Turks a new fortified city was built – Tvrđa with powerful fortifications, a series of Baroque barracks and the main square with the City Sentinel, the General's quarters, the Magistrate halls, while in the middle of the square the Baroque circular pylon of the Holy Trinity and a fountain were built. The Jesuits built the parish church of St. Michael with two belfries while the Franciscans erected a monastery and the church of the Holy Cross on the location of the one time mosque. With some Biedermeier houses, the Osijek Tvđa has preserved to present days its Baroque appearance although the main part of the fortifications were pulled down in 1923.

The Osijek Lower City took shape along the Drava river as a settlement for merchants and craftsmen. The Upper City developed in the fastest manner and from the 19th century it became the center of the integrated city. The buildings that stand out are the classicist palace of the county, the neo-Gothic parish church of St. Peter and Paul frequently colloquially

Osijek, Tvrđa, the square of the Holy Trinity, the building of the main command (1726) and Kužni pil (1730)

Below: Osijek, motif from Tvrđa   *Right: Osijek, neo-Gothic parish church of St. Peter and Paul*

Osijek, the interior of the parish church of St. Peter and Paul

Right: Osijek Art Nouveau, a residential building on Europe avenue

Below: Osijek, Europe avenue

called "the cathedral", the theatre building and a number of historicist edifices. Numerous Art Nouveau residential houses, the Art Nouveau building of the cinema "Urania" and the main post office endow the center of Osijek with a special value. Osijek is a city of parks with well thought-out horticultural solutions. New settlements rose radially around the center but also around the well-kept promenade along the Drava river. Osijek lost its former strategic importance already during Austrian rule when the border with the Turks was stabilized on the Sava river. Although during the period of the Austro-Hungarian monarchy Osijek was one of the most powerful industrial centers within Croatia, with the ending of Austrian rule but especially between the two world wars when the main

Osijek, Gallery of Figurative Arts, Master of "Vukovar Landscapes", Threshing, around 1850.

thoroughfares passed through the Sava valley, Osijek found itself on the sidelines and it began to stagnate. Today Osijek is an important industrial center, a significant university city and the planned construction of the highway from Hungary to the Adraitic via corridor across the Drava river promises that it will have a greater transportation significance.

The Đakovo region

Đakovo lies to the south of Osijek. In the 13th century it was mentioned as Dyaco, the property of the Bosnian bishop. A cathedral with the bishop's residence stood along the fortress. The settlement alongside the army camp dates from the 14th century. Due to Turkish destruction only a capital and a small part of the defensive wall have been preserved. After the expulsion of the Turks in 1687 the settlement began to be restored. As an interesting site one can mention the Turkish mosque which was transformed into the Catholic parish church of All Saints with the addition of a historicist façade. The core of Đakovo was shaped during the late Baroque period. The famous Croatian politician and patron of

Osijek, Gallery of Figurative Arts,
F. Amerling, Portrait of Alvina
Hilleprand-Prandau 1852.

The painted interior of the cathedral in
Đakovo

Left: Đakovo, the bishop's residence　　　　　　　*Above: Cathedral in Đakovo, view of the cupola and the main apse*

the arts, the bishop of Đakovo, Josip Juraj Strossmayer had the monumental three nave cathedral of St Peter built (1866-1882) in the neo-Romanesque manner in the very center of the city. A high cupola (54 meters) stands at the junction of the longitudinal naves and the transept while the façade is flanked by two belfries 84 meter high. The interior of the cathedral has been richly painted by the followers of the German "Nazarenes" painters. The Đakovo cathedral is the symbol of the city, visible on the Slavonian plains from a great distance. The Baroque bishop's residence was extended in the 19th century. A significant collection of artworks is located in the salons of the residence.

Baranja

Baranja spreads out northeast of Osijek in the triangle between the rivers Drava and Danube and the Hungarian border. Croatian Baranja is the southern part of historical Baranja whose larger part is a part of Hungary. Baranja is a flatland and its highest elevation, hill Bansko brdo does not rise above 250 meters. In the area where the river Drava flows into the

Danube there is a wooded and swampy space which is one of the richest zoological and botanical preserves in Croatia so that in 1967 it was proclaimed a natural park.

The largest town in Baranja is Beli Manastir followed by Darda and Bilje. Baranja is largely an agricultural area. At the end of the 17th century in the area of Bilje a large agrarian holding was put into operation in the ownership of the famous military commander, count Eugene of Savoy which was during his lifetime one of largest and the most developed agrarian holdings in Europe of that time. On its foundation in the recent past the large agricultural-industrial complex "Belje" has been built. Renowned vineyards lie on the slopes of the hill Bansko brdo while in the settlement Kneževi Vinogradi we find the famous wine cellars dug into the mountain.

Western Srijem

The area of western Srijem bordered by the rivers Dunav and Vuka on the north, the border with Serbia to the east, the river Sava to the south and the stream Jošava to the west spreads to the east of Osijek.

Vukovar, Franciscan monastery and the church of St. Philip and Jacob (18ᵗʰ century)

Vukovar, the interior of the church of St. Philip and Jacob devastated during the last war

Ilok, Medieval walls and the church of St. Giovanni da Capestrano

Vukovar

The main center of this area is the city of Vukovar which stands where the Vuka flows into the Danube. The area around Vukovar has been inhabited since the Neolithic period. On the locality Vučedol on the Danube near Vukovar an archeological site of a Copper Age lake-dwellers culture has been excavated, especially richly endowed with excellent ceramic artifacts. Under the name Vučedol culture it has become a part of the inventory of the heritage of ancient Europe as one of the most important prehistoric complexes. A settlement within the area of Vukovar has certainly been in existence since the 10th century. Medieval Vukovar was composed of three parts: the Fort with the city, the army camp Walkow on the right side of the Vuka , the outskirts which received the status of the free royal city and the city on the left shore of the river Vuka. During the Turkish occupation sacral and other buildings were destroyed and Vukovar became a typical small town with about two hundred houses. After the end of the Turkish occupation the restoration of the city began during the Baroque period. From 1730 it became the feudal holding of the Eltz family. The city was given a Baroque appearance. The Franciscans built an important monastery complex and the church of St. Philip and Jacob. At the beginning of the 20th century the church and the monastery were encircled by gardens. The parochial Orthodox church of St. Nicholas was also done in the Baroque style. During the middle of the 18th century the count Eltz family built a large early-classicist castle while the administrative building for Srijem county is also a fine example of Baroque classicism. A number of historicist buildings such as the synagogue done in the Moorish style were built in the 19th century. The most monumental historicist building in Vukovar is the neo-Baroque building of the hotel "Grand", later transformed into "Worker's hall" on the very shore of the Vuka river. At the beginning of the 20th century Vukovar saw the rise of a series of buildings done in the Art Nouveau spirit. Between the two world wars the Czech industrial magnate Bata built in the vicinity of Vukovar , in Borovo, a large rubber-shoe plant with a well planned settlement for the workers. During its most productive years it employed up to 20.000 employees.

Vukovar was almost totally destroyed during a three months siege in the last Homeland War when more than 6000.000 different bombs and grenades exploded on the city. Today it is being gradually rebuilt, virtually out of ashes.

Vinkovci, a view of the banks of Bosut river

Vinkovci, the old city center

Ilok

Ilok, the easternmost Croatia city is located on the banks of the Danube river, in a place which since Antiquity has been a favorable crossing across the river. Partially it stands on an elevation along the Danube river while parts of the city rise onto the slopes of Fruška gora hills. The Medieval fortress Vylak was a powerful and large fortified city which loomed over the Danube. Of the several churches that stood within the confines of the fortress, the church of St Giovanni da Capestrano along with the Franciscan monastery has been preserved. In the 18th century Ilok was turned into a large feudal holding of the famous family of the counts Odescalchi. To the west of the Ilok fortified city, the Odescalchi built a large two-storey castle with a park which was renovated a number of times during the 19th century. Located on the slopes of Fruška gora hills the Ilok region is renowned for its vineyards and high quality wines.

Between the rivers Bosut and Sava

To the west of the Srijem cities, on the river Bosut, lies Vinkovci, a regional center which particularly developed after the building of the railroad line and it thusly became the

Slavonian riders

Slavonian swine-herds

Gorski Kotar landscape

main railroad junction of eastern Croatia. To the south, on the easternmost tip of Posavina is Županja, once an important center of the Croatian Military Border and today the junction of roads especially of the important one which leads to Bosnia and further towards the Adriatic coast.

MOUNTAINOUS CROATIA

Mountain Croatia is definitely, because of the configuration of the terrain, the most sparsely populated part of Croatia but its importance lies in the fact that it is a linking space between middle Croatia and the Croatian Adriatic coast. All of the more important historical roads made their way through this space. The construction of the railroad line to Rijeka and afterwards towards Split has particularly added to the significance and value of this area. Today, when two modern highways from Karlovac to the Adriatic (to Rijeka, Zadar and Split) have been constructed this area gains more and more in importance, particularly because of its natural beauty and its almost untouched nature which has increasingly become a tourist destination. Mountain Croatian consists of the northwestern parts of the Dinara mountainous space. It is divided into Gorski Kotar, Ogulin (or sub-Kapela) valley and Lika.

The Gorski Kotar region

Gorski Kotar consists of the massifs of the high mountains of Bjelolasica, Risnjak and Snježnik. Amongst the mountain massif we find smaller separate fields and land extensions in the Karst terrain. The rivers Kupa, Dobra and Čabranka flow at its edges. The passes through which roads used to pass are shallow so that for the modern highways long tunnels had to be dug. The first significant transit routes were built in the 18th and the beginning of the 19th century – the roads Karolinska cesta (Charles's and Maria Louise' s road) and Lujzinska cesta towards Kraljevica and Rijeka while the railroad line Budapest-Zagreb-Karlovac-Rijeka was built though Gorski Kotar in 1873.

Smaller settlements and market places such as Delnice, Čabar, Skadar, Ravna Gora and Vrbovsko came into being during this period. Since Gorski Kotar is predominantly a forest area, the systematic exploitation of woods and plants for its processing began in a number of the said settlements.

The natural beauty of the region and its relative proximity to large centers such as Rijeka and Zagreb make Gorski kotar a particularly attractive tourist zone.

A national park was declared on the locality of Risnjak mountain especially to protect its specific forest flora and fauna.

Ogulin, parish church of the Holy Cross from 1781.

during the period of the Croatian Miltary Border when a settlement with a regimental command was built around the fortress. Ogulin is the largest settlement in Mountainous Croatia. It underwent a significant process of development when, after the abolition of the Croatian Military Border, it developed a wood-processing industry. Today it is becoming a tourist destination.

Lika

Lika is a Krast basin bordered by Mala kapela, Velebit and Plješevica mountains and the flow of the river Una which is the state border with Bosnia and Herzegovina. The significance of this area particularly lies in the possibility of establishing traffic routes in the north-south direction so that throughout history this has played a great role. During the 18th century, the one time caravan routes were transformed into imperial roads which from the interior made their way to the Adriatic harbors. The construction of these roads was enabled by the terrain which in its central area is relatively low hills crisscrossed with smaller Karst fields alongside the flows of numerous Lika rivers. This area is exceptionally rich in water so that if it were not for unfavorable historical circumstances which have brought about a depopulation of Lika , some of its parts, if they had employed all the natural resources, could have been a Croatian Misira. The largest water courses in Lika are produced by the three largest rivers – Gacka, Lika and the Krbava river. The westernmost river is the Gacka and

Area around the city of Ogulin

The foothills of Velika and Mala kapela, the mountain range which forms a natural barrier between middle and central Croatia, are called the Ogulinska and Potkapelska valley. During the Middle Ages the main settlement was Modruš. It developed alongside a Frankopan burgh from the 12th century. Up to the 16th century it was a secular and religious center with a bishop's seat. The incursions of the Turks in the 16th century destroyed the significance of Modruš. Ogulin developed alongside a fortified city from the 15th century raised over Đulin chasm on the Dobra river. It became significant

Brinje, Sokolac burgh, the Gothic chapel of St. Mary

Velebit, Zavižan

Gospić, city public gardens

Above: River Lika   *Below: The birth place of the famous Croatian 19ᵗʰ century politician Ante Starčević*

its valley is the largest. The strategically most significant settlement in this area is Otočac located on the western part of Gacka valley. The Medieval fortress from the period of the Croatian Military Border was one of the fulcrum points of the defense of the road between the sea and the continent. The construction of the road Jozefinska cesta (Josephine's road) from Senj towards Karlovac at the end of the 18ᵗʰ century contributed to the significance of the Gacka region. Lika is the longest Croatian intermittent river(78 kilometrs). Together with the waters of the Gacka river, its waters were used when the Senj hydro-electric power plant was built. In the Lika valley a new Lika center rose – Gospić which became particularly important when the road Marijaterezijanska cesta (Marie Therese's road) from Karlobag across Baške Oštarije to Gospić was built. Subsequently the administrative offices were removed from Karlobag to Gospić. During the 1920s a railroad line was constructed from Zagreb to

On the next pages: Motifs from the National park of Plitvice lakes

Split through this central area of Lika. Today's modern highway follows the same direction. During the 1970s, more to the east, along the river Krbava the main road between Dalmatia and Zagreb was constructed. This road passes through the spacious Krbava valley under the town of Udbine and passes over into Korenica valley and afterwards through the

Above: Under the Great Waterfall

Left: In the mirror of Prošćansko lake

Dried-out waterfall at the beginning of Galovac

area of Plitvice lakes along the course of the river Korana to Karlovac. The westernmost and the shortest railroad line runs along the border with Bosnia and Herzegovina along the course of the Una river.

During the Middle Ages the Lika region was settled while numerous fortified cities protected the local areas and roads. The incursion of the Turks during the 15th century into these areas made this space the place of decisive defense. According to contemporary chronicles, in the famous Krbava battle almost the entire Croatian nobility was killed, with the Croatian Vice-Roy at the head of the army while in the struggle with the soldiers of Jacub pasha several thousand warriors met their death. During the 16th century Lika was a constituent part and one of the most important sectors of the Croatian Military Border bordering the Ottoman empire. The haphazard living conditions lasting for a number of centuries left a deep mark on the entire area. It is only with the recent building of modern highways that there is hope of putting to an end

the process of depopulation. One of the most important components of new developments lies in tourism.

The Plitvice Lakes National Park

On the northeastern rim of Lika lies the most famous and doubtlessly most beautiful Croatian national park and the most significant tourist destination in Lika – Plitvice lakes. This area of exceptional beauty is composed of 16 larger and smaller lakes within the area between Mala Kapela and Plješevica. Surrounded by hundred year old forests the clear lakes fall and flow across gypsum barriers into one another (the height difference is 134 meters). In such a manner numerous larger and smaller falls and cascades are formed. The Plitvice area abounds with other attractions such as caves and an exceptional rich plant and animal life. The clear, green river Korana flows out of the falls and into the river Kupa nearby Karlovac.

LITTORAL CROATIA

Along with the abundance, wealth and diversity of the continental area, the Croatian Adriatic coast with its size, morphology, ancient historical contacts, its heritage and its natural beauty is the most dominant phenomenon of such a small country. Covering by far the largest and the most indented part of the eastern Adriatic shore and lying in the northwest-southeast direction it stretches out for almost 800 kilometers. The actual length of the coast itself is 1777,3 kilometers while the coastline of the 1246 islands, islets and sea-cliffs is 4058 kilometers long. The total of 5835 kilometers of coastlines is surrounded by more than 30.000 square kilometers of territorial sea. When these impressive numbers are compared with only 56.000 kilometers of the Croatian land mass, the significance of the littoral and the centuries-old attempts by foreigners to conquer it become obvious. The Croatian Adriatic coast is certainly the most powerful factor contributing to the importance of Croatia as a country.

The Croatian littoral is divided into the northern littoral with Istria, Kvarner and the area under Velebit mountain and the southern part which encompasses the old historical region of Dalmatia.

Istria

Geographically speaking, Istria can be defined as a peninsula whose northern land border is formed by the line between Miljski bay (Muggia) in the immediate vicinity of Trieste and the northernmost point of Prelučki bay, to the northwest of Rijeka. Its southernmost point, the tip of the peninsula is cape Kamenjak southeast of Pula. The Istrian peninsula is the largest and the most important example of the indentation characteristic of the Adriatic coast. The gravitation to centers to the west and to the east of Istria created variegated political, economic and cultural lines of force on Istrian soil throughout the centuries so that the explanation of the course of its history and of culture is more complex then a simple geographical definition can offer. Even the very structure of the morphologically different geographical wholes in Istria contributes to the complexity of explaining Istria as a unified geographical concept.

From its hinterland land mass Istria is divided by limestone mountains and the hilly highlands of Trščanski Kras, Ćićarije and Učka. The space of the peninsula can be divided into three geo-morphologically wholly different areas.

Because of its scarce vegetation and bare and light Karst surfaces the hilly northern and northeastern rim of the peninsula is called While Istria. The part of this area which is made up of mountain Učka falls steeply into the sea so that the littoral population of the eastern part of the Istrian peninsula has always been turned to the sea and the maritime life while in the more recent past it has taken up tourism.

To the southwest of White Istria a morphologically richer

Vineyards in Motovun

space spreads out. This is a hilly region crisscrossed by river courses and valleys, rich in water and vegetation. Although the soil is not particularly rich, throughout the centuries the production of cereals, fruit, vineyards developed here and large livestock was raised. Since this area is characterized by deciduous vegetation, during the winter months gray color dominates the area so that the region is called Gray Istria. Since prehistoric times settlements have been founded here on elevated places or on hills which dominated over the rivers and the fields. On the foundations of numerous prehistoric hill forts, citadels, Antique and later fortified Medieval fortified towns came into being. In this region even many villages have their fortification walls. Gray Istria had abundant layers of coal so that in its southeastern part, especially in the area of Raša and Labin, so that there was a long tradition of mining which has today died out.

The southern and western coast of Istria is characterized

Novigrad stands on the very place where the river Mirna flows into the sea

98

by a broad belt of flatland which gently slopes to the sea. The coast is indented with numerous coves and deeper bays and with river deltas. Along with a series of smaller islands, the Brijuni archipelago stands out in front of the shoreline from Poreč to Rovinj. The whole region has retained a covering of red earth so that this area is called Red Istria. The area is relatively densely populated and along the western coast of Istria we have a number of smaller cities such as Umag, Novigrad and Vrsar. In Red Istria agricultural production is highly developed while significant industry has developed in the urban zone of Pula. Today the whole coast of Red Istria is an important tourist area, one of the most significant and the most developed tourist zones in the Republic of Croatia.

The greatest part of the territory of Istria, in fact the entire corpus of the Istria peninsula south of the delta of the river Dragonja all the way to the top of Prelučki bay to the north-

Scene from Buje

east, is a constituent and vital part of the Republic of Croatia. Croatian Istria encompasss the dominant part of White, the greater part of Gray and the entire area of Red istria.

Istria has been settled from ancient days which is testified to by numerous findings. During the Iron age Istria was densely populated by Illyrian tribes. The Histri tribe inhabited its largest area and the entire peninsula has acquired its name from this tribe. The Japodas, an Illyrian-Celtic tribe, inhabited its northern, rim areas while the eastern part of the peninsula, from the delta of the river Raša, belonged to the Illyrian tribe the Liburnians. The entire area of Istria is covered by remnants of Libernian hill forts and first Roman and afterwards Medieval cities and settlements were built on many of these. Roman colonization began in the 2nd century BC and continued slowly along with strong resistance from the Illyrians. They set up their colonies in Pula (Pola), Poreč (Parentium) and Labin (Albona). During the Roman period, the southern part of Istria with its center in Pula was particularly densely settled.

The eastern Goths ruled Istria during the early Middle Ages while from the 6th to the 8th century it was under Byzantium authority. Indirectly through the Aquila patriarch, German emperors held sway over Istria up to the 15th century when the whole of Istria, excepting the Pazin dukedom and the Kvarner littoral, came under Venetian rule. This rule lasted almost four centuries. The Habsburgs inherited Pazin and the Kvarner littoral. After the fall of Venice and after the Napoleonic wars, Istria was under Austrian imperial rule up to WWI. Between the two world wars Istria belonged to the Italian monarchy and during this period, especially during the time of fascist repression, an exodus of Croatian population took place. After the capitulation of Italy in 1943 Istria became a part of Croatia according to decisions reached already during the war. It was finally liberated in the spring of 1945.

With its picturesque towns and a series of other attractive seashore settlements the western coast of Istria is exceptionally attractive to tourists. In the interior of Istria we find a generally hilly terrain whose prominent elevations are dominated by smaller picturesque towns. A cultivated landscape, tilled soil and numerous vineyards, avenues of trees, woods and water courses are constituent parts of an exceptional space that many have compared with Toscany.

Poreč

The city of Poreč dominates the area from Tarski bay in the north to Limska Draga (cove) in the south of the western Istrian coast as well as the greater part of the interior of the peninsula, almost to its center. It is considered a very old city and is one of the historically and monument-wise most important urban centers in Istria. Built as an urban center during the Roman period, Poreč has managed to preserve the basic typical Roman urban grill pattern with a main longitudinal street (decuman) and a transversal thoroughfare (kard) . Remains of

Poreč, Euphrasius' basilica, the preserved original stucco works from the 6th century on the arches of the northern arcades

the temple have been preserved within the area of the forum. Medieval Poreč has been preserved in numerous Romanesque and especially Gothic buildings. As the seat of the one-time

Left:
Poreč, the complex of the Euphrasius' Basilica.
View of the roof of the octagonal baptistery (6th century).
Atrium of the Euphrasius' basilica (6th century)

Figures of bishop Euphrasia, archdeacon Claudio and his son Euphrasia on the mosaic of the central apse (6th century)

bishopric, Poreč has preserved valuable sacral monuments of which the complex of basilicas of the bishop Euphrasius from the 6th century have to be pointed out. According to its architectonic conception but also according to the style of its mosaic paintings, Euphrasia's edifice is a work of Byzantium art from the period of the great emperor Justinian. Even in its present shape, Euphrasia's basilica is an exceptionally harmonious edifice with an elegant arcading and refined relationship of space and its wall masses. Brilliant mosaics with a gilt background in the apses highlight this harmony focusing one's attention on the space of the ritual. Owing to its exceptional

complexity, the state in which it has been preserved and its extraordinary artistic and historical significance, the entire Episcopal complex in Poreč, whose core is the basilica of bishop Euphrasia, in 1996 was included in the UNESCO inventory of world artistic heritage.

On the coastal part of western Istria one's attention is drawn by Limski bay. This is an unusual geo-morphological phenomenon that came into being by the flooding of the lower part of Limska Draga (cove) into a 10 kilometers long and 500 meters wide sea bay whose shores steeply climb into the air over a 100 meters. Progressively becoming narrower, in the interior of the land it is transformed into a dry Karst valley which up to Kan-

far lies in the east-west direction and then suddenly turns towards the north to almost 5 kilometers near Pazin. At intervals the stream Lim flows through the valley. This Karst phenomenon probably came into existence on the site of the one time river Pazinčica which today is an underwater river. Together with the bay the entire length of this valley is over 35 kilometers. For centuries the long Karst valley was the main route for all the traffic that took place from the western coast of Istria towards its interior. Limski bay itself is a very picturesque bay whose shores are overgrown with evergreen shrubbery. Today it is a tourist attraction while in its upper part one nowadays will find fisheries and the shell-growing farms.

Left: Rovinj, view of the historical city center

Rovinj, picturesque Baroque houses on Novi trg (new square)

Rovinj, the Baroque Balbi arch raised in 1680 on the site of the onetime city gate

From old Rovinj

Rovinj

To the south of Limski bay on an indented shore with numerous coves and smaller islands stands Rovinj, one of the most beautiful and picturesque towns on the Adriatic coast.

The position of the historical core of the city of Rovinj on an smaller peninsula which juts out into the sea between two deep coves contributes to the atmosphere of spatial harmony. The high buildings of the old city which almost from the level of the sea climb towards the top of the hill form a homogenous tissue of picturesque, narrow and winding streets clustered on the hill like a clenched fist. The top of the mountain is crowned by the large horizontal of the church of St. Euphemia. This horizontal line is partially softened by the greenery of the trees while the final compositional touch is produced by the monumental belfry which projects high into the sky. The vertical line of the tall buildings is emphasized by the numerous picturesque chimneys that decorate the Rovinj roofs.

The old town is somewhat separated from the newer quarters on the land by an isthmus on which stand a number of spacious Baroquely defined squares and streets built within the belt in front of the town walls and on a location which in part was created by the filling in of the sea. The newer parts of the city built in the 18th and the 19th century spread out harmoniously like a fan into the two Rovinj coves. The green forested island of Saint Catherine gives a special atmospheric touch to the southern Rovinj cove.

Vodnjan, one of the largest centers of southern Istria, is located some twenty kilometers north of Pula. Surrounded by olive groves and the vineyards of the fertile Istrian flatland, the city rises on a gentle slope, recognizable by its monumental urban structure but especially by the high belfry of its parish church of Saint Blaž which reaches high into the sky.

Large Brioni island, remains of a sumptuous Roman summer house

Brioni, the remains of a large fortified building called "the Byzantium castrum" in Dobrika bay on the western side of Large Brioni island.

Brijuni National Park

The Brijuni islands, one of the true Istrian pearls, are located almost on the very northwestern exit from Pula harbor. The group is made up of two larger islands, Large and Small Brijun, and 12 islets. Only the 3 kilometers wide Fažanski canal separates them from the Istrian shore. They were inhabited as early as prehistoric times while they were considered particularly attractive during the Roman period when in the entire area of southern Istria summer landholdings with luxurious villas were built. Without doubt the most luxurious is the complex of the summer castle in Veriga bay built in the 1st century BC. The excavated remains of this complex spread out on an area of approximately five acres. Life on Brijuni lasted throughout the Middle Ages as well as during the Venetian administration but it was brought to a stop due to malaria in the 18th and the 19th century. Moving its main navy base from Venice to Pula, in the second half of the 19th century, Austria on Brijuni built seven powerful fortresses, of which the largest was fort "Tegetthoff" on the hill Vela straža on Large Brijuni. When it was being built it was one of the mightiest forts on the Mediterranean. In 1893 the Austrian industrialist Paul Kupel-wieser bought the Brijuni islands and before WWI transformed the dilapidated area into one of the most fashionable and attractive summer resorts. From 1947 the islands became the official summer residence of Josip Broz Tito and remained so until his death in 1980. During this period, new luxurious hotels were built and parks, meadows and the Brijuni woods restored and enriched. During this period Brijuni islands were visited by the most eminent world politicians while a number of historically important political meetings were staged there. Since 1983 the Brijuni islands have come under protection and now have the status of a national park.

Pula

Pula is the largest city center on the Istrian peninsula. The city is located at the top of an indented and deep bay which

Right and above:
Pula, view of the Roman amphitheatre

Right and below:
Pula, the peripheral wall of the amphitheatre has two rows with 72 vaults each and 64 square openings near its top

Pula, the City hall and Augustus's temple on the site of the onetime Roman forum

position has always given it the significance of being a good harbor and a secure anchorage. Owing to its dimensions and location, the islets in the bay which divide the harbor area into a number of basins, as well as because of the excellent approach from the open seas and the possibility of easily fortifying the shores, even today in maritime science the harbor of Pula is held to be one of the best and the safest natural harbors in the world.

The city arose on a fort-hill Illyrian settlement which was located on a hill overlooking the bay (today the citadel). After 177 BC Roman rule was established. Roman Pola had a spacious forum with temples and accompanying buildings. Augustine's temple and the famous Sergijevaca arch derive from the early Roman period. The city had two theatres, the smaller one inside the city walls while the larger was built to the south of the city. To the northeast of the city in the immediate vicinity of the city core in the 1st century a large amphitheatre was built, the sixth according to size amongst those which have been preserved in the world today and which could hold more than 20.000 spectators. Its arena was used for gladiator fights and other widespread Roman entertainments for the populace. As early as the 4th century Christian places of worship were built in Pola while the Pola cathedral of St. Mary was built in the 5th century. The city began to rapidly develop from 1866 when Pola became the main

Augustus's temple on the Pula forum

Façade and belfry of Pula cathedral

Pula, the preserved southern chapel of the basilica of St. Mary of Formosa

base for the Austrian imperial navy. The development of Pola during the period of the Austro-Hungarian monarchy was really intensive. Starting with barely a few hundred inhabitants at the beginning of the 19th century, the population of Pola before WWI grew to 60.000. Cosmopolitan Pola from the period of the Empire collapsed in 1918 while between the two world wars, having lost its strategic significance, it barely subsisted as an administrative center under Italian rule. Today it is the most important ship building center in Croatia, a strong tourist destination and a university city. Today the famous Roman arena is the center of cultural events, ranging from operas, great concerts and a famous film festival.

Interior of Istra

With its old towns and settlements, the interior of the Istrian peninsula bears witness to the thousand years old cultural tradition of this space since there is hardly an inhabited place where one will not find valuable monuments of architecture and art or at least interesting environmental phenomena. It needs to be said that in the 15th century there developed in Istria an intensive painting activity largely by native masters who decorated the small sacral buildings with specific late Gothic paintings which, frequently alluding to distant examples, have an irresistible charm of a sort of folk art. Such

Sveti Lovreč Pazenatički, apses of the parish church of St. Martin (11th century)

preserved frescos have made famous the churches in Oprtalj, Hum, Pazin, Beram and Žminj while those in Sveti Lovreč Pazenatiči and those nearby Peroj display valuable remains of wall paintings from the 11th and the 12th century. The specificity of smaller Istrian churches is the covered portico in front of the building which enabled the folk to attend the Mass despite the restricted space. Such a portico in Istria is called the lopica.

On the extreme northwest in the hinterland of Umag stand Buje which is even today an important center which has managed to preserve its historical urban core, the grill of narrow streets and the picturesque quality of its environment.

Right: Oprtalj, view from the air

Sveti Lovreč Pazenatički, Romanesque-Gothic tower-bell-tower. To the right the apses of the parish church of St. Martin from the 11th century.

Motovun situated itself on a hilltop from which it domintes the valley below.

A number of historical towns stand alongside the course of the river Mirna on the surrounding hilltops. The Medieval fortified towns of Grožnjan and Oprtalj stand over the right side shore of the Mirna river. On the left shore of the river Mirna, on a steep height (277 meters) which dominates over the valley stands the picturesque town Motovun. Buzet, once a Venetian military headquarters sits astride almost the center of the northern part of Istria, under the massif of Ćićarija and in the immediate vicinity of the source of the river Mirna.

Hum, the famous Glagolithic center, because of the urban character of its architecture and its organization, but also because of its pronounced miniature dimensions has been designated by the epithet "the smallest city in the world". Sveti Lovreč Pazenatički is located some ten kilometers inwards to the southeast of Poreč and is renowned for its valuable Medieval architecture while Sveti Petar u Šumi is known for its Benedictine monastery from the 13th century which was taken over by the Paulists in the 15th century. The

Žminj, Baroque parish church of St Michael

Istrian continental center is Pazin and is today the center of the Istrian region. All three Istrias meet in the Pazin area – the White, Gray and Red Istria so that throughout history Pazin has played an important role. It was the feudal center of the Pazin dukedom and from the 14th century it was under the rule of the Habsburg empire. The foundation of the feudal seat of power is the powerful Citadel which was built on a steep cliff over the Fojba, the hollow into which flows the river Pazinčica, the only underground river in Istria. The present appearance of this powerful fortress dates from the 16th century.

Nearby Pazin on a steep ridge of a hill stands Gračišće, today, sad to say, partially desolate, with really comely examples of Gothic architecture (the Salamon palace).

Svetvinčenat stands amidst a woody elevation in the eastern part of the dry-land part of the Rovinj area. Along with its complexes of interesting secular and sacral architecture, the most significant architectural whole is the Gothic citadel

Gračišće, the porch of the church of St Mary on the Square with its Baroque wooden cassetted ceiling

The lane of Glagolitic writers Roč-Hum, Želimir Janeš: "The Rise of the Istrian Divide" nearby Hum (1980)

Left: Gračišće, view from the air

Below: Sveti Petar u Šumi, the cloister of the Pauline monastery

118

Bale, the Soardo-Bembo citadel with Gothic quadroforia (14ᵗʰ-15ᵗʰ)

Left and above: Žminj, fresco from the 14ᵗʰ century in the chapel of St Anthony

Left and below:

Beram, detail of a fresco showing the Dance of Death (1474.)

Žminj, detail of the fresco in the chapel of St Anthony

Right: Entrance into the Pazin Citadel

Soardo-Bembo, impressive in its serious monumentality but also in the beauty of its two-story quadriphoras.

In the immediate vicinity of the Raša river-mouth stands Barban famous for the unusual complex of the Loredan palace which in the early Baroque period was incorporated into the earlier built citadel whose northern part was rebuilt as a parish church in the 18ᵗʰ century. Every year Barban hosts the game of chivalry called "Race on the ring" which is very similar to the tilting at the ring tournament (alka) in Sinj.

Svetvinčenat, view from the air

Raška bay and the coast beneath the Učka mountain massif

On a strategic position, on a ridge of the elevation which separates Raški bay from the eastern shore of Istria stands Labin, in Roman times known as the Albona camp, and during the early Middle Ages one of the first Istrian cities to come under Croatian rule. During the Venetian period it became a very important and fortified strategic locality. Labin abounds in fine examples of patrician palaces from the Renaissance and the Baroque period, of which the representative palace Battiala-Lazzarini from the first part of the 18th century, one of the best preserved original Baroque palaces in Istria, stands out.

The old city of Plomin stands over the relatively deep and narrow Plomin bay which was created during the period when the river Boljunčica still flew into the sea in this place. Today its flow disappears in the nearby Ćepić-Polje.

In Antiquity Plomin was known as Flanona so that it gave its name to Kvarner bay – Sinus Flanaticus. Picturesque, huddled high over the bay, endowed with an interesting architecture, today it is almost deserted.

Right: Scene from old Labin

Labin, façade of the Baroque Battiala palace - Lazzarini from the 18th century

Right: Opatija hotels

The eastern shore of Istria is characterized by high steep shores by way of which the Učka massif descends to the sea. Settlements are rare and those such as Brseča, Moščenica and Veprinac stand high over the sea. The space where the mountains are a bit more gentle creates a thin belt of shoreline which enabled the building of settlements. During the period when tourism began in the 19th century it was this area where winter and health resorts were built for the rich clients of the Austrian empire. In time this area became the most famous destination within the monarchy so that the construction of hotels, health resorts and stately villas spread from Opatija to Lovran giving shape in such a manner to the famous Opatija Riviera. In the period after WWII the international popularity of this destination enabled an even more intensive construction of tourist facilities which spread even to the one time smaller fishing settlements of Ika and Ičići between Lovran and Opatija. Today this area is one of the most significant

Opatija, villa Angiolina

Croatian locations particularly because the gentle climate, the beauty of the landscape, numerous excursion sites, the luxuriant and comfortable architecture of the hotels, the well-groomed parks and promenades along the sea, along with all other urban amenities, make possible a tourist season which lasts the whole year.

Kvarner islands and the Croatian littoral

Rijeka

Rijeka, the third largest city in Croatia and the largest Croatian sea harbor, is located in the northern part of Rijeka bay. The location of the city in a place where the Adriatic makes the deepest inroads into the Middle European land mass determined the destiny of its development as the dominant harbor with all the accompanying features such as shipbuilding, the processing industry and trade. Although as an urban center it developed relatively late, Rijeka is an old city. As far back as Illyrian times the Illyrian hill-fort Darsata,

later the Roman fort Tarsatica, stood on the high rise over the sea. During the Middle Ages the citadel on Trsat was fortified and enlarged under the powerful feudal family the Frankopans. During the Middle Ages, along with the feudal citadel on the elevated terrain, a settlement with all of the accompanying Mediterranean characteristics developed along the river Rječina which after the church of St. Vid was called Reka of St. Vid. The city on the sea began to grow during the Baroque 17th century. Rijeka went through a process of rapid development after the great earthquake in 1750 after which the city was restored and enlarged. The authorities of the times decided that the growth of the old city turned to the canal of the river Rječina cease and that the new city quarters be turned directly to the seashore. The demolishment of the city wall created the façade of the city while the old city belfry received a new, more luxuriant Baroque appearance including a monumental city gate. The shore was gradually filled in, new blocs of luxuriant residences were built in the spirit of Baroque classicism while a new trading harbor was built on the city shore. The most luxuriant preserved space is the interior of the administrative building of the one time large sugar refinery. The Korzo in Rijeka was constructed as a spacious longitudinal promenade which is separated from the city harbor by the southern complex of buildings. The

Left and above: Rijeka, cathedral of St. Vid

Right and above: Trsat, the church of Our Lady of Trsat

Left and below: Rijeka, interior of the cathedral of St. Vid

Right and below: Icon of Our Lady of Trsat

Left and above: Rijeka, Modello palace, southern façade
Left and below: Rijeka, the palace of the Philharmonic
Orchestra, sculptures of the muses on the façade
Below: Art Nouveau façade of a building on the street
Korzo in Rijeka

Rijeka, the Croatian national Theatre I. Zajc

nineteenth century with its industrialization, better sea and land links and with the later railroad connections additionally contributed to the development of the city. Extensive filling up of the water expanded and deepened the space of the harbor while the construction of two large breakwaters divided this space into the western and the eastern basin. After the Hungarian-Croatian agreement in 1867 Rijeka received the temporary status of a Hungarian harbor and this "tentative solution" endured up to the fall of the Austro-Hungarian empire in December 1918. During those fifty years the development and the expansion of Rijeka were truly impressive. Showing in its own manner its political power and the growing supremacy over the Austrian part of the dual monarchy, Hungary through investments in the Rijeka region sought in every respect to be equal to Trieste, the central Austrian harbor. The construction of large palaces on the

Sculpture of the Croatian composer Ivan Zajc

Rijeka, Fountain and the Rijeka "Skyscraper"

Rijeka, palace at the seafront

seafront, a new square with the imposing theatre building, the new luxurious Governor's palace, the railway station building and numerous other buildings done in the historicist neo-styles gave Rijeka the appearance of a wealthy Middle European city. Maritime trade, shipbuilding, industry and trade grew in multifold fashion as well as the number of the inhabitants. According to the Rapallo agreement after WWI Rijeka along with the surrounding area became an independent tampon mini-state between Italy and the Kingdom of Serbs, Croats and Slovenes to be shortly afterward occupied by Italian extreme paramilitary forces under the command of the famous poet G.D. Annunzio. With the coming of the fascist to power the informal occupation was turned into official annexation. The city was divided into two parts along the river Rječina. The city itself came under the rule of Italy while the outskirt district of Sušak with the accompanying harbor facilities was a part of the Kingdom of Serbs, Croats and Slovenes. After WWII Rijeka became the main harbor of Yugoslavia as well as a transit harbor for the countries of Central Europe. It was then restored and expanded especially eastward towards the basin of Bakar bay. Today Rijeka is a modern and vital city at the junction of European corridors. In addition to its dominant economic significance it is an important cultural and university center. Retaining in its appearance and to an extent in its mentality some quantity of its earlier pronounced cosmopolitanism, Rijeka today represents the natural Croatian entrance door to Europe and a significant link between the Mediterranean and Middle Europe.

Bakar

In the immediate vicinity of Rijeka is the deep and spacious Bakar bay at whose bottom on a shallow elevation stands the old, picturesque, maritime city of Bakar. At the very exit from Bakar bay lies Kraljevica, built in the 18th century as a royal harbor during the rule of the Austrian emperor Charles IV where the so-called Charles's imperial road from Karlovac to the sea ends. The Old and the New City of

Bakar, the old city center

Novi Vinodolski

Vinodol

the Zrinski dukes dominates the city. The old city was built above the harbor in the 17th century while the new city was raised by Petar Zrinski at the entrance into Bakar bay as a fortified castle having a rectangular ground plan with four cylindrical towers at the angles.

Vinodol is an area that spreads eastward from Bakar bay. It consists of a narrow littoral belt above which rise ridges which in the continental area are transformed into a valley with a number of fields (Tribaljsko and Velo) which subsequently climb in a steep manner towards Gorski Kotar. The

Crikvenica

Senj, the Renaissance Nehaj fortress

Vinodol area was a possession of the Frakopan dukes, one of the most powerful feudal families. The cities of Crikvenica and Vinodol stand out on the narrow littoral belt. For a long period of time Crikvenica was a harbor for a Vinodol interior settlement but it became a tourist-health spa destination at the end of the 19ᵗʰ century. Today tourism has determined the character of not only Crikvenica but also of the larger settlements in the Vinodol area, especially Novi Vinodolski which stands on the exact place of contact between the Vinodol valley and the shoreline. The city grew alongside a Frankopan citadel. The city prides itself with the Vinodol Book of Law from the 13ᵗʰ century, one of the oldest and the most important Medieval legal documents in Croatia. The coastline continues under the ridges of Velebit mountain and is the most sparsely populated area of the entire Croatian shore.

Senj

Of the settlements one must mention the city Senj which during the era of sailing was one of the most significant Croatian harbors. A very old settlement dating back to Illyrian times, Roman Senia was already strategically important as a

place where the caravan routes descended from Pannonia to the sea. Senj takes pride in its 12th century Romanesque cathedral. During the wars with the Turks the city had a decisive strategic role so that in the 16th century its military command was the embryo of the Croatian Military Border. Although the city was fortified and had a citadel, an important role in the defense of the broader area was played by the Renaissance fortress Nehaj built in 1558 on an elevation over the city. The famous Senj "uskoci" (runaways), by organizing arms attacks on Turkish territory, played an important role in the defense of Croatian space. From 1772-1779, during the reign of the Austrian emperor Joseph II, the so-called Charles's road was built which connected Karlovac with Senj over Vratnik pass. From that point in time the importance of Senj as a harbor significantly grew. The later more favorable orientation of transporting goods to the harbor in Rijeka, especially with the attendant rise of steamships, annulled the significance of Senj as a harbor.

Karlobag

To the southeast of Senj one must mention Karlobag, a town which was historically important for the littoral beneath Velebit mountain. During the Middle Ages, named Bag, it was a possession of the powerful Croatian noble family Kurjaković. It was burned in 1525 by the Turks but less then 50 years later it is recorded as Karlobag after the name of the archduke Charles Hapsburg who put together the first serious defense against the invading Ottoman forces. In the 18th century it was connected by way of the so-called Maria Therese road across Baške Oštarije with Gospić in Lika and was in this manner given the role of a transit harbor for goods coming from the interior. The Velebit littoral continues to the mouth of the Zrmanja river but already before Starigrad it enters the gravitational area of the Dalmatian region.

The sea area which in the west is bordered by the south-ernmost tip and the eastern shore of Istria, by Rijeka bay and the Vinodol and the sub-Velebit littoral creates the spacious Kvarner bay whose surface is covered with large inhabited islands: Cres and Lošinj facing the Adriatic open sea and Krk and Pag turned to the landward side of the bay.

Islands of Cres and Lošinj

In reality Cres and Lošinj form a unified whole since the isthmus which naturally links them has been dug up and connected by a movable bridge. Cres is sparsely populated. The city Cres, a very old settlement, was founded in Roman times under the name Crespa. It lies along the shore of the deep Cres bay. During Venetian rule it was the administrative center for both islands.

The oldest urbanized settlement on Cres is Osor. During both Antiquity and the early Middle Ages, antique Apsoros was an important center, the seat of a bishopric and a Benedictine monastery. With the coming of the Venetians it lost its

Above: Osor, the cathedral

Cres, the village Lubenice

Mali Lošinj

function and rapidly declined. Small island settlements were frequently built on the very ridge of steep mountains. Of these the most picturesque is Lubenica from which a magnificent view of the open Adriatic sea can be had. In the middle of the island is the large fresh water lake Vransko jezero which is the natural reservoir of drinking water for both Cres and Lošinj. One of the attractions of Cres is the habitat of the griffon, a rare, preserved species of an almost extinct bird of prey.

Lošinj is a high woody island whose main center Mali Lošinj with its 6300 inhabitants is the largest settlement on the Croatian islands. The town owes its growth to the rapid development of shipping and the maritime trade in the 18th and the 19th century. A typical urban settlement with its frugal but dignified architecture it stands at the bottom of a deep bay. Already as early as the end of the 19th century health tourism began to develop in Mali Lošinj equally as in the nearby Veliki Lošinj. Today these are places which are strongly oriented to tourism but they have also retained their status of being climatic health spas. In the open seas before Lošinj lies an unusual island – Susak, covered with deep layers of sand. Susak is known for its unusual woman's garb with its very short skirt and a number of underskirts which wholly cover the legs clothed in long purple socks.

Veli Lošinj

Island of Krk

Krk is the largest island on the Croatian Adriatic sea. It was settled from oldest times. During the Roman period the greatest concentration of settlements was located around the present city of Krk. With the coming of the Croats, settlements rose in all parts of the island whose flatlands and fields provide conditions for agriculture and stock-breeding. Settlements on strategically important places developed on the shoreline. During the Middle Ages it was a possession of the Frankopan dukes who brought to the island people from the Velebit area. The northern part of the island is sparsely populated and is in large part an infertile heath. The Rijeka airport has been built on this location while a large oil terminal has been built in Omišalj from whence pipes reach Hungary. In 1980 Krk by way of the islet of St. Mark was con-

Krk, city fortifications and the church of Our Lady of Carmelite

Right: Vrbnik

Krk, pre-Romanesque church of
St. Donatus in the bay Puntarska uvala

Krk, the Romanesque church of
St. Quirinus adjoining the Krk cathedral

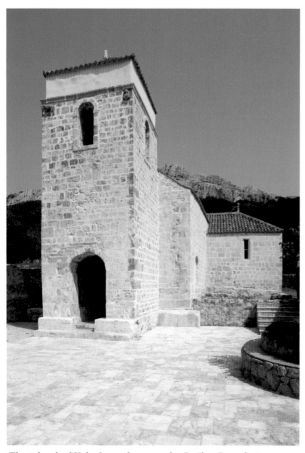

The island of Krk, Jurandvor nearby Baška, Benedictine abbey church of St. Lucia, beginning of the 12th century

Košljun, cloister of the Franciscan monastery from the 16th century

nected by two concrete arch bridge constructions with land. In recent times these changes have brought about the situation that the island has been closely integrated into the broader

*Jurandvor, St. Lucia,
Baščanska ploča- section of the altar railing*

zone of the city of Rijeka. The island itself is full of picturesque settlements and numerous cultural monuments, significant works of art and archeological sites which cannot be discussed in this brief account. Krk is one of the centers of Glagolithic literacy. In Jurandvoru, in Baška Draga nearby Baška, in the Benedictine monastery church of St. Lucia, the famous Baščanska ploča (plate) was discovered. Once a part of the altar railing on which is to be found a long Glagolithic inscription from the 11th century it is in reality a bequest made by king Tomislav to the monastery of St. Lucia. The plate is one of the oldest carved monuments to the Croatian language. The Franciscan monastery on the islet Košljun in the middle of Puntarska cove is renowned for its written Glagolithic documents but also for its other important collections.

Island of Rab

Rab lies opposite to the sub-Velebit littoral, forming with its northeastern shore a part of Velebit canal. The northern

134

Rab, the preserved sections of the city wall on the southern part of the peninsula

Rab, the church and Benedictine convent of St. Andrew, 11th-18th century

part of the island, exposed to the frequent squalls of the northern wind, is desolate and rocky while the central part of the island is protected by the ridges of Kamenjak rise. Several fertile fields around Supetarska draga, Kampor and Banjol provided the basis for settling the island. The main settlement on the island is the historical city Rab. One of the most beautiful coastal cities, it stands on a peninsula which encloses the indented bay. The settlement dates from Antiquity but its rise

Rab, city loggia

Rab, bell-tower of the church of St. John the Evangelist, 12th century

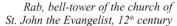

Rab, Romanesque façade of the cathedral of St. Mary the Glorious, 12ᵗʰ century

took place during the Middle Ages when it became the seat of a bishopric and a free city commune, well-fortified by walls within which are to be found many exceptionally important and valuable buildings, especially from the Romanesque period when the city was at its heights. What creates the characteristic and the exceptionally picturesque silhouette of the city are the high and slim belfries of the churches in Rab and the preserved remnants of the walls. The main sacral monuments are located on the topmost ridge of the peninsula amongst which are the one-time Rab cathedral of St Mary the Great, then the early Romanesque basilica of the Benedictine convent of St. Andrew with a belfry from 1181, the Benedictine monastery church of St. John the Evangelist from the 11ᵗʰ century and its belfry from the 12ᵗʰ century and the Renaissance church of St. Justine. The prince's castle, the belfry with the city watch, the city loggia and a number of valuable residential buildings such as the palaces of the Dominis, Nimira, Crnota, Galzigna and the Marinelis families stand out amongst the public buildings. The early Romanesque church of St. Peter from the 11ᵗʰ century, raised alongside the Benedictine monastery in nearby Supetarska cove, is significant for the study of Medieval architecture and construction.

Island of Pag

Pag is a borderline island which because of its position and large length intrudes into Kvarner bay, with its northern shore encloses the southern side of Velebit canal and with its eastern part is linked with the area of Dalmatia with which it connected by a bridge. As with all of the inner islands alongside the sub-Velebit littoral, the northern side of Pag, exposed to constant northern wind and salt spray, is wholly desolate. All of the settlements are turned to the south except the city of Pag itself which lies at the protected bottom of the deep Pag bay. The history of Pag is particularly interesting. As Pag bay, stretching in the southeast direction, ended up on a long longitudinal shoal ideal for the construction of saltworks, the old city of Pag stood on a gentle slope more than two kilometers to the southeast of today's city. The old city of Pag was heavily destroyed in the battles with people from Zadar at the end of the 14ᵗʰ century. Since salt was one of the strategically most important articles, the Venetian administration decided to offer better protection to its saltworks so that in 1443 it ordered a newly fortified city of Pag to be built at the very entrance into the shoals. Its regular square foundations, partially protected by walls, might have be drawn up by the

Pag, façade of the choir church

famous builder and sculptor Juraj Dalmatinac. Within the walls, the city consists of a geometrically uniform grill of streets. At the junction of the longitudinal and the vertical street there is a rectangular square with the main church, the

Right: Attire worn on the island of Pag

Pag, remains of the citadel

prince's castle and the bishop's palace which was never completed. Salt warehouses of which the oldest date as far back as the 14th century lie to the southwest of the city. The other island settlement of the urban type, Novalja, lies to the northwest of the island. During Antiquity the area of present Novalja was the southern harbor of the Roman city Cisse (today Caska) in the northwestern corner of Pag bay. Numerous findings bear witness to the fact that during the period of the rise of Christianity and during the early Midle Ages life within this area was very intense. Today's Novalja is primarily a tourist center. With its urban arrangements and with an abundance of residential and summer house architecture, with its well-kept streets, parks and its shore, Novalja is an example of a cultivated relationship to space. The island of Pag is renowned for its sheep raising and the production of the most high-quality cheese. The most intensive production of this article for which there is a great demand takes place in the area of Kolan in the central part of the island.

DALMATIA

Dalmatia, the southernmost Croatian region, stretches from the broad area of the mouth of the river Zrmanja to the peninsula Oštro at the entrance into Boka Kotorska bay. This is an elongated littoral belt lying in the northwestern-southeastern direction, its longitudinal axis more than 400 kilometers long while its greatest width in its central part does not exceed 70 kilometers. Towards the continental area the space is bordered with high mountains – the southeastern part of the Velebit massif and the mountain chains of Dinara and Kamešnica while in the southeastern area this natural mountain bulwark is significantly lower. The 926 islands, islets and sea cliffs are a special treasure of the Dalmatian littoral belt. Some of these, such as Brač, Hvar, Korčula, Dugi otok and Mljet belong amongst the largest Adriatic islands.

In contrast to the opposite Italian, the Adriatiac shore which is almost without protection, the chain of islands alongside the Dalmatian coast shape sheltered sea canals very favorable for navigation along the coast which was exceptionally important during the era of sailing. In such a way, since from of old, a strategically important Adriatic route was established over which regional and even world maritime powers engaged in conflict.

Four larger rivers have their mouths on the Dalmatian coast – Zrmanja (64 kilometers), Krka (75 kilometers), Cetina (105 kilometers) and Neretva (218 kilometers) along whose courses fertile fields were formed. This is particularly true of the broad valley formed by the Neretva delta with its 12 tributary streams. Two larger natural lakes, Vransko jezero and Prukljansko jezero in the broadening of the lower course of the river Krka, are to be found in the Dalmatia region. The artificial lake Peručko over the dam of the hydro-electric plant on the river Cetina is the largest water accumulation in Croatia. The Karst lakes such as the Modro (blue) and Crveno (red) jezero nearby Imotski and Baćinska lake in the hinterland of Ploče contribute to the attractiveness of the Karst area.

A Mediterranean climate with long, dry summers and gentle, relatively rainy winters is characteristic of the Dalmatian area. The vegetation, dependent on climatic conditions and the characteristic Karst terrain is typically Mediterranean, especially luxuriant and variegated in the middle and the southern area. Because of the configuration of the terrain with the specificities of mountain massifs and high plateaus, continental Dalmatia has a intermediary, sub-Mediterranean climate.

The present population of Dalmatia is about 900.000 inhabitants with a strong concentration around its regional centers, Zadar and Šibenik in the northern part, Split with its broader littoral area in central Dalmatia and the city of Dubrovnik in the far Dalmatian south.

After a long period when its transit routes were simply insufficient, today Dalmatia, as a region emphatically turned

On the sea

the Roman incursion into their areas, the name of their tribe became a synonym for all the Illyrian tribes which lived within the littoral area. Roman rule was finally consolidated in this region when emperor Octavian Augustus in 9 AD put down the great Illyrian rebellion. The name Dalmatia came into use from the 2nd century for the greater part of the one-time Illyrian area. In the geographical sense this was a much larger territory than that signified by the contemporary term and its size varied according to the political circumstances in the Roman Empire. The capital city of the province was Salona, a large cosmopolitan city whose remains are to be found around the present city of Solin nearby Split. Many rulers came and went in the turbulent history of this area. During the rule of the East Roman emperor Justinian in the 6th century this region was a Byzantine province. In the 7th century, during the Avar-Slav onslaught, a large number of Dalmatian cities were destroyed, amongst them Salona itself. The Byzantine possession was reduced to a number coastal cities with Zadar as the seat. What characterized the end of the 8th and the 9th century was the expansion of the Franks into these areas and the slow strengthening of the Croatian state in the

The belfry of the Split cathedral as seen from Diocletian's palace

to tourism, is becoming more intensively and in a more modern manner integrated into the flows of contemporary traffic. Its final highway integration with the continental part of Croatia and in such a way with international traffic corridors became an imperative ever since Croatia became independent. This is especially reflected in the completion of a modern highway which links the region with the network of modern highways with their junction in Zagreb and with the construction of a longitudinal highway which will be a part of the future international highway corridor leading to Greece.

The name Dalmatia dates from the middle of the first century BC and derives from the Illyrian tribe Delmata (Dalmata) who inhabited the area between the rivers Krka and Cetina. In the old Illyrian language Del or Dalm meant shepherd which defines stock raising as the basic occupation of the tribe. Because the Delmata put up the strongest resistance to

The central triforium of the Sponza palace

coastal hinterland. In the 11ᵗʰ century the Croatian king Petar Krešimir IV held the title of king of Dalmatia and called the Adriatic his sea. After the fall of the Croatian national dynasty Dalmatia was ruled by Hungarian-Croatian rulers. During dynastic intrigues for usurping the Hungarian-Croatian throne, in 1409 king Ladislav of Naples sold Venice his royal rights to Dalmatia for 100.000 ducats. Because of continuous threats from the Turks and Venetian-Turkish wars, the land borders of Dalmatia oscillated depending on the fortunes of war and agreements amongst great powers. After the fall of the Venetian republic, during the Napoleonic campaigns, Dalmatia was for a short period of time under Austrian and afterwards under French rule. In 1813-1814 it again found itself under the rule of the Austrian empire. From the Vienna Congress in 1815 up to the destruction of the Empire in 1918, Dalmatia was a region under the Austrian crown. After WWI Dalmatia found itself a constituent part of the Kingdom of Serbs, Croats and Slovenes but because of the ill-fated treaty with Italy in Rapallo it had lost its once capital city Zadar and the island of Lastovo. After WWII the space of Dalmatia made up a constituent part of Croatian territory within the framework of new Yugoslavia. During the war for the independence of Croatia between 1991-1995 the territory of Dalmatia underwent severe damages, especially its hinterland area while the coastal cities, especially Zadar, Šibenik and Dubrovnik, were systematically targeted. But the wounds have healed and Dalmatian cities again glitter with the beauty which has been built throughout the centuries and millennia.

Northern Dalmatia

Sights of nature

There are a number of natural attractions within the northwest Dalmatian area which because of their exceptional geographic morphology, the intactness of their natural environment and their unusual beauty draw intermittent attention. Accordingly, some have been declared by law protected areas, three national parks, a number parks of nature and protected landscapes.

Velebit, Velika Paklenica

Paklenica National Park

The first and the oldest within the Dalmatian area is the National Park Paklenica founded back in 1949. It is located on the southeastern rim of the Velebit massif and it is composed of two deep and steep canyons which have been cut into the mountain massif by Velika (large) and Mala (small) Paklenica. Numerous sightseers and tourists are attracted by the climb through the canyons and a favorite challenge to mountain-climbers are the gigantic vertical rocks of which the most impressive is the one called Anića kuk, 712 meters high. NP Paklenica abounds in underground Karst phenomena. Of the registered seventy odd caves the most famous is Manita peć (175 meters long), unusually rich with cave decorations. The entire Velebit massif has been proclaimed a natural park. Tulove grede over the canyon of the river Zrmanja stands out with its dramatic beauty in its southeastern part. The clear green river makes its way through the high winding canyon to the broadening into the body of seawater Novigradsko more to finally make its way through Novsko ždrilo into the sea.

Starigrad-Paklenica, the church of St. Peter, 11th-12th century

Krka National Park

The course of the river Krka, the second Dalmatian river which has its source under the craggy Dinara mountain, on its way to the sea brings a wealth of natural phenomena but just as many significant cultural historical locations so that in 1985 more than two thirds of the river course was proclaimed a national park. From its source, Krčić fall under Dinara mountain to its joining the sea it displays different morphological characteristics: deep canyons, falls and cascades, gypsum barriers, wide spaces that are almost lakes, the mighty fall at the lower part of its flow before it levels out with the level of the sea and stilled in such a manner makes its way across the flooded Karst field and through the winding

Right: River Krka, the fall Skradinski buk

Visovac monastery on the river Krka

canyon reaches the waters of Šibenik harbor. In the upper course of the river Krka, nearby Ivoševac stands the famous Orhodox monastery Anađelovac, a valuable cultural monument. Between the barriers of Roški fall and the seventeenth cascade of Skradin fall is an elongated river basin in whose

141

center is the islet Visovac with a church and a Franciscan monastery surrounded by gardens. The hermits of St. Augustus founded it in the 14th century but they fled before the Turkish threat. In 1445 Bosnian Franciscans inherited the holding and survived there under Turkish rule.

Where the Krka becomes placid, beyond the bent of the great waterfall, lies the picturesque town Skradin, Scardona in the antique period, a place of special significance.

Vransko jezero natural park

Between the rivers Zrmanja and Krka, almost alongside the seashore, lies lake Vransko jezero, in reality a large flooded Karst field whose shores are overgrown with canes and swamp grass which create a natural nesting place for a great number of swamp birds. Today it is a well-known ornithological preserve and recently it has been proclaimed a park of nature.

Kornati National Park

The Kornati archipelago, a stone necklace of larger, smaller islands and sea cliffs lies dispersed in the open sea almost opposite of lake Vransko jezero. With almost 150 islands on a relatively small territory the Kornati are the most indented and the densest island group on the Mediterranean. The islands got their names from the cliffs on the outer chain

Above: The crown on Kolobučar

Left: Kornati islands, garma, a steeply indented bay

and from their specific geological forms which resemble crowns atop the islands. Thusly the Kornati are in reality "crowned islands". From old times sheep were raised on the islands from which they did not move. Every owner on an island had his temporary modestly made shelter. Stock raising on the islands affected the putting up of a complex labyrinth of walls, partitions and barriers built with drystone walls which today cover the islands like some sort of unfathomable "land art". It is this primordiality of human action in nature which is a constituent part of the value and the purpose for preserving this territory.

Because of the specificity of the landscape, the variety of Karst phenomena, the endemic flora, fish breeding grounds, the ornithological community of sea birds but also because of the specific role of man in the shaping of this unique phenomenon, it was necessary to protect this exceptional area from devastation and unhampered exploitation so that in 1980 it was proclaimed a national park. The space of the deep and

143

Left and above: Kornati,
land enclosures in the port Pod Bižanj

Left and below: Kornati, small olive grove

Right and above: Kornati, Islet Zornik

Right and below: Koromašnja port on Kornati

144

Kornati, the island Mali Obručan

Knin fortress

indented shore of Telaščica on Dugi Otok which with Kornati constitutes a unified area was designated in 1988 a separate park of nature. Of the three chains of Kornati islands, two are protected by the borders of the national park and encompass 101 islands. The Kornati islands are generally the property of the inhabitants of the island of Murter.

The Northern Dalmatia hinterland

The land part of the area of northern Dalmatia which spreads out between the river Zrmanja and Krka, in its north-western part at the foothills of the rims of Velebit mountain, is the rocky, almost fruitless high plateau of Bukovica where only some stock breeding could develop. The town of Obrovac, once a fortified city of the Kujaković dukes of Krbava, developed as a market place on the left shores of the Zrmanja river. To the east the rocky high plateau rises into the high mountains of Dinara and Svilaja and amongst them, like an island, hovers the lonely mountain of Promina. The valleys between the mountains, alongside the courses of the Krka river and its tributary stream Čikola, expand into fertile fields which were the basis for the growth of larger settlements.

Knin

Knin as an important center at the crossroads of roads from old times represented an exceptionally strategically significant place. The dominant elevation on which the Medieval Knin castrum was raised controls the ford across the Krka river. Many Croatian kings from time to time had their seat in the city of Knin. Its location, the complexity of its walls and fortresses as well as what they held made this fortification system one of the largest and the most impressive in the continental part of Dalmatia.

Otavice near Drniš, family Mausoleum of the famous Croatian sculptor Ivan Meštrović

Drniš

Drniš stands under the hill Promina at the very top of the spacious Petrovo field and is today the center of a rich agricultural area while formerly it was a fortress of import during the Venetian-Turkish wars. In nearby Otavice is the mausoleum of the Ivan Meštrović family where the most famous 20th century Croatian sculptor was buried in 1962.

Ravni Kotari

The southern, most spacious part of the northern Dalmatian land mass which descends to the coast is called Ravni Kotari, a flatland with only a number of elevations. Owing to its morphology and the composition of the soil it is the most fertile part of the entire Croatian littoral. Therefore it does not come as a surprise that in history this area was inhabited by many peoples, from the Illyrian tribe the Liburnians to Roman settlements in Antiquity. This is the area where the Medieval Croatian state took shape. Because of this rich hinterland and the strategic roads that passed through this terrain, as early as Antiquity the city of Zadar developed on the

147

Nin, the church of the Holy Cross, 9ᵗʰ century

shores of Ravni Kotari. It is one of the historically most significant Croatian littoral cities. Not far from it stands Biograd na Moru, the city where kings were crowned and one of the seats of the Croatian medieval state.

Nin

As far back as the Roman period, the city Aenona (Nin) develped in the western part of Ravni Kotari in a shallow, swampy lagoon. It was destroyed during the Slav-Avar incursions during the early Middle Ages. At a later date Nin was restored and from the 9ᵗʰ century this was where the castle of the Croatian rulers was located and the seat of the Croatian bishop. From this period the most significant, up to the present day preserved, monument is the small church of the Holy Cross, an edifice having a circular ground plan with a cupola. The wider area of Nin and the seashore all the way to Zadar is a developed tourist zone.

Benkovac

The center of the agricultural-economic zone of Ravni Kotari is the city of Benkovac, in the 15ᵗʰ century the center of the Croatian dukes Benkovići around which a market place eventually developed. In its immediate vicinity one can view the locality Aseria, in the Illyrian period a powerful hill-fort with cyclopean walls and during the Roman period a fortified castrum with all the features of Roman urban architecture.

The northern Dalmatian littoral

Biograd na Moru

A number of settlements along with the city Biograd na Moru are located on the relatively low, approachable shore of the Zadar littoral. Today a pronouncedly tourist locality, it played an important role in the history of Croatia. It was built and fortified on a small peninsula in the 9th and the 10th century. From its beginnings it belonged to the Croatian ethnic and cultural base. It was the seat of the Sidraška county and in the 11th century the capital of the Croatian king Petar Krešimir IV and the seat of the bishopric. At the end of the 11th century the Croatian king Dmitar Zvonimir held court in the city. In 1102 king Koloman from the Hungarian dynasty Arpadović was crowned as the Croatian king in the church of St. Thomas of the Benedictine convent. Biograd was totally destroyed when the Venetian fleet attacked it in 1125 and never afterwards did it regain its one time glory.

Zadar

Zadar is the urban, economic, cultural, educational and tourist center of the broader region within the area of northern Dalmatia. Although according to size it is the fifth city in the Republic of Croatia it represents one of the most significant Croatian urban centers.

Zadar, the façade of the cathedral of St. Anastasia

its role to Zadar. The city gradually developed into a powerful Medieval community whose economic and political power aggravated the enmity of its competitors, especially Venice.

Venice ruled over Zadar for almost four centuries. Because of the growing Ottoman threats, the capital of Venetian Dalmatia, under the leadership of its best military builders, was transformed into the most powerful Venetian fortress on the Adriatiac coast. Never conquered, after the fall of Venice it first, for a short period of time, was under Austrian rule, afterwards under the rule of Napoleon's military forces to finally function as the capital of the Kingdom of Dalmatia under the Austrian crown for more than a century.

According to the ill-fated peace treaty in Rapallo in 1920 it was given to the Kingdom of Italy together with Istria, Rijeka, the islands of Cres, Lošinj and Lastovo. Separated from its motherland and its people it existed for two decades as a free port. During WWII it underwent catastrophic bombardment during a dozen continuous air attacks by the Allies. Reunited with

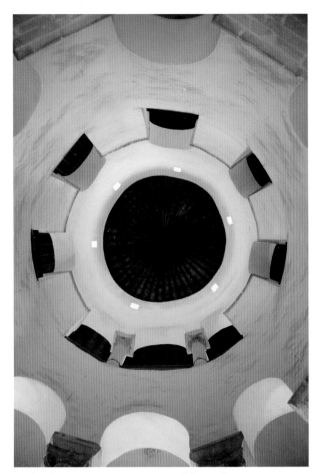

Zadar, St. Donatus, interior, view of the roof

The Illyrian settlement that was located on the space where Zadar stands dates from the 8th century BC. In the 7th and the 6th century BC, Idassa was already an important center of the Illyrian tribe the Liburnians. The Roman conquest and the gradual settlement of the Zadar area coincides with the period when Caesar conquered Illyricum in the 1st century BC. During the time of emperor Augustus at the end of the century it had already risen to the status of a colony under the name Colonia Julia Iader. This was already a Roman city built according to plan with all of its secular and cult functions, encircled with firm fortifications. During the period of the growth of the Christian cult it built significant edifices on whose foundations during the Middle Ages the Episcopal complex was constructed, without doubt one of the most significant on the eastern shores of the Adriatic. During the Middle Ages Zadar had a dominant role among the Dalmatian cities. The destruction of Salona devolved

Left: Zadar, the church of St. Donatus, 9th century

Zadar, St. Mary, monastery church of the Zadar Benedictine nuns. The bell-tower was built by the first Croatian-Hungarian king Koloman in 1105. The façade of the church was renovated in the Renaissance manner in the 16th century

Zadar, permanent Exhibition of Religious Art,
"Benedictine Madonna", around 1300

complex which today encompasses the largest Dalmatian cathedral, a harmonious Romanesque edifice from the 12ᵗʰ and the 13ᵗʰ century, consecrated to the Srijem Martyr woman St. Anastasia. There is also the renovated baptistery from the 6ᵗʰ century but above all the famous rotunda of St. Donatus, the most famous early Medieval building monument in Zadar. In its rough monumentality and with its proportions it stands out in its originality. Opposite to the Episcopal complex stands the convent church of the Zadar Benedictine nuns consecrated to the Virgin Mary. The church of this influential convent was built in the Romanesque manner at the end of the 11ᵗʰ century but was thoroughly renovated in the middle of the 15ᵗʰ century according to Renaissance mores. The capitulary hall of the convent has up to the present day been preserved in the original Romanesque form. Alongside the church stands a monumental Romanesque belfry which was raised by the Hungarian-Croatian king Koloman in 1105.

In 1972 on the earth surface where stood part of the convent of the Benedictine nuns of St Mary that had been destroyed in

Zadar, Franciscan monastery, miniature
from the antiphonary, 13ᵗʰ-14ᵗʰ century

the homeland after the war it went through a long period of restoration and today has developed into a modern and attractive city.

What makes Zadar particularly distinct are its building monuments and the enormous artistic and historical wealth preserved in its significant museum institutions, libraries and archives. Alongside the excellently presented remnants of the largest Roman forum on the eastern shore of the Adriatic and the historicist archbishop's palace rises the monumental Episcopal

Zadar, Franciscan monastery, Ivan Petrov from Milan, Ugljan poliptych, 15th century

WWII, two winged building were built. These buildings housed the Permanent Exhibition of Religious Art , one of the major objects of Croatian culture, opened to the public in 1976.According to the number, artistic value and the significance of the artistic items this collection of religious art has no equal in Croatia. The time span covered by the exhibited artworks is more than a thousand years, from the 8th to the 18th century.

The Archeological Museum was founded in 1832 and as such is the second oldest Museum institution in this part of Europe. The collections of this Museum, covering the period from prehistory to the early Middle Ages, do not only have a national relevance but many exhibits are important for European heritage as such.

A significant collection of artworks, especially those dating from the high Middle Ages and the early Renaissance, are in the possession of the monastery of St. Francis.

Of the many other significant monuments one must mention the Romanesque church of the one time monk's monastery of St. Chryogonus from the 12th century and the church of St. Simeon which dates from the 5th century but which underwent numerous renovations and extensions all the way up the Baroque period. Within it are kept the relics of St. Simeon in a famous gilt silver coffer, the gift of queen Elisabeth born Kotromanić, the wife of the Hungarian-Croatian king Louis the Great Angevin.

Of the secular monuments the ones that stand out are the

Zadar, church of St. Simon, silver gilt casket for the body of St. Simon. Made in Zadar by the goldsmith Franjo from Milan between 1377-1380 as a gift for queen Elizabeth the wife of the Hunagarian-Croatian king Ludovic I, House of Anjou.

pentagonal Captain's tower from the 13th century, the late Renaissance city loggia and the City watchtower but especially the Land Gate for which the design was made in the middle of the 16th century by the famous Venetian architect Michele Sanmicheli.

Zadar has a Scientific library which is the second largest in Croatia, a State Archive which stores exceptional rarities as well as some of the most important documents pertaining to national history. The University in Zadar takes pride in its 600 years tradition.

The sea in front of Zadar has a variegated archipelago and the numerous larger and smaller islands are clustered in front of the Zadar land mass in three island chains. The first chain consists of the islands Ugljan and Pašman while the outer chain is closed by Dugi Otok. Silba, Olib and Permuda are the most distant islands to the northwest while to the southeast the Zadar islands conjoin the Kornati archipelago and through this group

the remaining islands of the Šibenik maritime area. A great many of the Zadar islands are inhabited while population is particularly dense on those nearest the shore. A number of significant Medieval monuments, particularly in Preko and Ugljan on the island of Ugljan, in Mali Iž on Iž, in Savar on Dugi Otok and in Kraj and Tkon on the island Pašman, are to be found on the Zadar islands.

Šibenik

Where the river Krka flows into the sea, the submerged river-mouth forms a spacious bay which is connected with the open sea by a deep, navigable canal. The city of Šibenik lies in this bay. Although a settlement existed here in Antiquity, Šibenik as a city rose during the Middle Ages. Šibenik finds

The Šibenik cathedral of St. Jacob, 15th-16th century

Above: Town-hall in Šibenik, 16ᵗʰ century

Right: Šibenik, the church of the Holy Salvation

Left: The Šibenik cathedral of St. Jacob, interior, 15ᵗʰ-16ᵗʰ century

first mention in a document from 1066 when it is explicitly stated that the Croatian king Petar Krešimir IV held court there during Christmas of that year. Thusly Šibenik is the most recently built of the Dalmatian cities and by all the evidence it was founded by Croatian kings, initially as a royal castrum. It is recorded that the Hungarian-Croatian king Koloman resided there in1105 and that during the 13ᵗʰ century it enjoyed the powerful protection of the Croatian dukes Šubići Bribirski. From 1298 Šibenik was a bishop's seat. From the 15ᵗʰ century, like the rest of Dalmatia, Šibenik was under the rule of Venice continuing in this position until its fall in 1797. The historical city of Šibenik, encircled by walls, developed out of three urban cores. The City occupies the central area around the cathedal and the townhall and spreads to the eastern part of the city walls. Gorica developed to the

Šibenik

north while the westernmost part, Dolac, developed around the oldest part of the harbor. It was only in the 19th century that the city began to develop outside the city walls and that it in time, like an amphitheatre, enclosed the bay from the west, north and east, spreading out in recent times outside the perimeters of the natural spatial whole.

The center of the historical city of Šibenik is its main square, Plathea communis, today the Square of the Croatian republic. On this square or immediately around it are located all the most significant secular and church buildings in Šibenik: the cathedral, the town hall, the city loggia and the prince's and the bishop's palaces. The surrounding area is full of numerous old Šibenik patrician palaces.

The Šibenik cathedral, consecrated to the apostle St. Jacob, is the most significant of the city edifices and its authentic symbol. Construction on it began in the 30ies of the 15th century and it was completed only in the second half of the 16th century. A number of generations of builders, sculptors and stone-cutters wove their best ideas and skills during the watershed period when the Renaissance gradually replaced the Gothic. Largely because of its famous builders Juraj Matej Dalmatinac and Nicholas of Florence and their bold decisions, because of the wondrous, almost organic interpenetration of styles but primarily because of the unique harmony of the completed whole, the importance of this edifice transcends not only the local or regional framework but offers an example how on the margins of cultures, in favorable circumstances and in the interaction of different generations, masterpieces deserving universal relevance can be created. With these characteristics the cathedral has been included in the UNESCO register of world artistic heritage. The old city core of Šibenik, in addition to a number of truly valuable

Primošten

Gothic and Renaissance church buildings, abounds with a number of picturesque small squares, an almost organic structure of streets and numerous patrician palaces with preserved portals, family coats-of-arm and other architectonic decoration. All of this endows this space with special value. Despite the destruction it underwent during WWII and a number of architectonic interpolations, the old city of Šibenik, as a few of the larger urban centers on the Adriatic littoral, has preserved its original environmental value.

The Šibenik littoral

A number of prominent tourist centers of which the most important are Vodice and Primošten are located on the coastal area of the Šibenik region. On the locality known as Bucavac nearby Primošten human hands have created vineyards by laboriously clearing stones and erecting regular rectangular drywall barriers in which at most two or three vine plants have been planted. The whole area is crisscrossed by these stone barriers so that a photo of this locality was exhibited in the United Nation building in New York as a homage to human labor. The famous Primošten red wine Babić is produced in these vineyards.

Alongside the Kornati archipelago which for the most part is a national park there are a number of inhabited islands in the Šibenik maritime area. Murter with its four settlements is the home island of the whole Kornati group where in addition to olive growing, stock-raising and fishing more and more people are turning to tourism. Even today the best wooden boats are made in Betina.

Zlarin is renowned for its corals, Krapanj for its sponges. Žirje and Kaprije are the most distant of the Šibenik islands.

Trogir, triforium on the large palace Ćipiko (around 1470.)

Left: Trogir and Kaštela bay

Central Dalmatia

Trogir

Trogir, one of the most significant and rich in cultural monuments cities on the Croatian Adriatic coast, lies at the northwestern entrance in Kaštela bay, at the place where the island Čiovo almost touches the land.

Trogir is not only one of the oldest urban centers on the Croatian coast of the Adriatic but with its four thousands year old history it can be enumerated amongst the oldest cities of the Mediterranean. First traces of organized life reach back to the prehistoric period around 2.000 BC. From this period one finds fortified settlements on the nearby hills surrounding the fertile field while the area of the present city itself on an islet which stands in a narrow canal between land and the island Čiovo seems to have been an organized settlement during the same period. The later Illyrian settlement after 219 BC became a market center of the important Greek colony whose center was on the island of Vis. Roman Tragurium developed during the 1ˢᵗ century BC. Already by this time the area around Trogir was known for its gold colored high quality marble so that the nearby quarries in large part produced the material for the construction of the decorative parts of the architecture in Salona and later for the representative segments of Diocletian's palace in the present city of Split.

During the Middle Ages, Trogir developed as a prominent municipality especially during the period of the Hungarian-Croatian rulers. For its princes Trogir chose members of the powerful Croatian noble families, especially the Šubići, which provided it with both protection and status. From 1420 to 1797 it was under the rule of Venice while during the 19ᵗʰ and the 20ᵗʰ century it partook in the destiny of the other Croatian cities. In the 15ᵗʰ and the 16ᵗʰ century Trogir was one of the most significant humanistic centers on the eastern Adriatiac coast. Amongst other things, during the Renaissance a very important literary circle using the Croatian language developed there.

Although Trogir lost the greater part of its Medieval fortification in the 19ᵗʰ century, nevertheless, the northern, land

Trogir, cathedral of St. Lawrence, main portal.
The work of master Radovan and his workshop

Trogir, southern shore

gate and the southern, sea gate with a part of the wall, the small loggia, the St.Nicholas tower and the Vitturi tower have been preserved. Of the fortifications on the western wall, the self-standing large citadel Kamerlengo (around 1450) and the round tower of St. Marc (around 1480) have been preserved.

The central city space was formed during the Middle Ages on the location of the Roman forum. The most important public and church buildings and the palaces of the eminent patrician families stand around the relatively spacious square. The Trogir cathedral of St. Lawrence, whose building began in the 13th century in the Romanesque mode, is the dominant edifice which dominates the square. Although it was completed by the middle of the 13th century, edifices were added to it along the northern wing up to the Renaissance period.

What makes the Trogir cathedral exceptional in the artistic heritage of Croatia is surely the Romanesque sculpture primarily expressed in the reliefs and statues of the main portal on its western façade. These are the works of master Radovan and of his workshop made around 1240 as the author himself testifies on an carved inscription in which he calls himself "most famous in this art". Going by the plasticity, liveliness and boldness of composition in those parts of the portal which

he himself cut, Radovan's sculpture can only be compared with the most significant works of European high Romanesque art.

In 1460 the sculptor and builder Andrija Aleši raised and decorated with reliefs in the northern part of the cathedral portico a baptistery inspired by the indented ceiling of Jupiter's temple in Diocletian's palace. In 1468 master Nicholas of Florence, pupil of the famous Donatella, began by opening a part of the western cathedral wall the construction of the chapel of Blessed John of Trogir, surely the most beautiful early Renaissance architectural and sculptural whole on the Adriatic coast. The exceptionally harmoniously shaped Renaissance space, vaulted over by a barrel-like indented ceiling is decorated with a number of extraordinary sculptures by Nicholas of Florence, Ivan Duknović and Andrija Alešija.

The city loggia stands opposite the cathedral. The first original building dates from the beginning of the 14th century but it was renovated in 1471 by Nicholas of Florence. A small three nave pre-Romanesque basilica of St. Barbara (11th century), originally consecrated to St. Martin, leans immediately on the southern wall of the city loggia. The entire western side of the Trogir main square is occupied by the late Gothic

Right: Trogir, central square with the Trogir cathedral of St. Lawrence, the town-hall, loggia and the complexes of the Ćipiko palace

Left: Kaštela bay   *Above: Kaštel Gomilica*

palaces of the eminent Trogir family Ćipiko.

Trogir stores numerous important objects and artworks in a number of significant monasteries and convents, in the city museum and in the pinacotheca located in the Romanesque church of St. John the Baptist.

Paying heed to the uniqueness of the urban core area, the high quality of the monuments of architecture and the preserved environmental values in 1997 UNESCO put Trogir on the Register of world cultural heritage.

The broader area of Split

The broad Kaštela bay under the mountain Kozjak opens up to the east of Trogir and this is the beginning of the wider agglomeration around the Dalmatian central city of Split. The broader area of Split consists of the city of Split itself, Solin and Kaštela but the continuous urbanized area spreads from the city of Trogir in the west to the city of Omiš to the east which is located at the place where the river Cetina flows into the sea. This long, but narrow, city agglomeration in whose center is the city of Split stretches out along the coastal belt for about 50 kilometers in length and 5 kilometers in width and encompasses Kaštela bay, the lower course of the river Jadro, the Split peninsula and the shoreline to the mouth of the river Cetina. Its continental hinterland is enclosed by the mountain

ridges of the Dinara mountains Kozjak and Mosor. The deep pass Klis is cut into this ridge through which from of old caravan routes connected the littoral area with the continental interior. From the direction of the sea, the island Čiovo can be included into this broadly conceived Split area. Owing to the high mountains this area is protected from the influence of continental weather so that the climate is very gentle and favorable for the growth of typical Mediterranean vegetation. A morphologically variegated, very functional and exceptionally attractive space, bounded by high mountains through which roads ensure communication with the interior, defined by a spacious and deep bay, sheltered islands and long massive capes, an abundance of healthy waters springing from the mountains, and by a belt of fertile soil along the shores of the bay, it was an attractive area to settle for all civilizations. This is proven by the rise and development of Roman Salona and afterwards by the construction of the large emperor's palace of one of the most significant amongst the Roman rulers, emperor Diocletian in the immediate vicinity of the city (today Split).

Kaštela

Kaštela is the common name for the seven exceptionally picturesque settlements in the littoral part of the broad bay between Trogir in the west and Solin to the east. The settle-

Solin, remains of the ancient Salona Roman amphitheatre

ments gradually developed around fortified buildings on the shore which in turbulent times already as far back as the 14th century, but particularly during the Turkish threat, had to protect the properties together with the populace which worked the fields. It was during the first incursions of the Turks into this area that the populace abandoned the villages on the mountain ridges of Kozjak and settled around the fortified citadels. Looking from the east to the west the Kaštela settlements are divided into the upper and the lower ones. Upper Kaštela include Sućurac, Gomilica and Kambelovac while the lower ones include Lukšić, Kaštel Stari, Kaštel Novi and Štafilić. In addition to the environmental value in Kaštela one can find a number of monuments of architecture from the pre-Romanesque to the Renaissance period. Locations from the time of the Medieval Croatian state such as the one in Bijaći where in the Middle Ages one of the temporary residences of Croatian national rulers was located are important findings in this area.

Solin

At the bottom of Kaštela bay today stands Solin which with its urban structure conjoins and is partially integrated into the northern parts of the city of Split. Going by the present state of its development and its large industrial complex it is difficult to imagine that in Antiquity on this relatively broad area Salona was located, a large cosmopolitan city which at the height of its glory at the end of the 3rd and the beginning of the 4th century, during the reign of emperor Diocletian, numbered according to estimates more than 60.000 inhabitants. Devastated at the beginning of the 7th century during Avar-Slav attacks it was never restored so that today it is the largest and the most significant archeological locality not only in Croatia but in the wider region. Interest in its remains have been recorded since the 18th century while with the rise of archeology in the second half of the 19th century it became one of the important European archeological locali-

Solin, the old Christian necropolis on Manastirine

ties, especially from the aspect of old Christian archeology. Archeological excavations which lasted for years have located and presented the most important urban complexes, such as the forum, basilica, the fortifications, the city gate next the theatre and the amphitheatre and the large necropolises. For world early Christian archeology of special interest are the three Christian necropolises with basilicas in the immediate vicinity of Salona – Kapljuč, Manastirine and Marusinac.

Croats settled nearby Solin in the 9th century alongside the river Jadro. On one of the islands in the mouth of the river Jadro, Medieval Croatian rulers erected two churches, St. Mary and St. Stephen of the island, probably mausoleums of Croatian kings. In 1896 the famous plate with the inscription by queen Jelena from the end of the 10th century was found on this location. The remnants of the early-Romanesque three nave basilica of St. Peter and Moses from the 11th century, in which in 1075 the Croatian king Zvonimir was crowned, are to be found a bit to the north alongside the right side of the Jadro river.

Split

To the east of Solin, standing on a separate peninsula around a spacious bay is Split, the largest city on the Croatian shore of the Adriatic and the second largest city after Zagreb in Croatia. Although there is evidence that the area of Split was settled at an earlier date, the city owes its founding and growth to two crucial facts. From 293 to 305 the famous Roman emperor Diocletian, the great reformer of the empire, himself by birth an Illyrian, probably born in Salona, built in a cove on the shore of the Split peninsula a huge palace, a fortified castle for which it has not yet been established whether it was planned as a new imperial seat on a strategically favorable locality or whether it was to be a summer residence in which the ageing emperor would spend his last years after leaving the throne. What is known is that in 305, after abdicating, he moved into the palace where he died in 315 and that he is buried there in a magnificent mausoleum. After Dio-

Split, Diocletian's palace, Peristyle

cletian's death the palace remained the possession of Roman emperors so that it is a known fact that the next to last emperor of the Western Empire Julius Nepot found shelter there in 475. The second event which was crucial for Split was the destruction of nearby Salona at the beginning of the 7th century when a significant number of survivors found shelter and eventually moved into the walls of Diocletian's palace. In such a manner Salona, dislocated, continued its life during the Middle Ages huddled amongst the walls of the emperor's palace. In time the significance of the of the new urban whole grew so that already in the Middle Ages Split expanded outside of the walls. Because of this its large western outskirts had to be fortified with walls and joined to the city within the walls. It was on this new city space that a spacious square was formed with buildings in the Gothic manner in which all the most important municipal institutions were housed. The city outskirts grew in a radial manner around the city which

Split, the Romanesque figure of the lion at the foot of the Split cathedral bell-tower. It is attributed to the sculptural workshop of master Radovan, middle of the 13th century

Under the belfry of Saint Duima cathedral

somewhat deformed rectangle. The longer sides are around 215 meters long while the shorter ones, the north and the south, are around 80 meters long. The entire surface of the complex amounts to about 30.000 square meters. It was built according to the architectural tastes and the ideas of the eastern part of the Roman Empire. All at once it represents a very luxurious imperial villa, a Hellenic city and a strongly fortified army camp.

In addition to the relatively well-preserved city gates, the corner towers and today finely presented wall paintings the most important preserved parts of the Roman palace are the Peristyle, a luxurious court yard bordered on three sides with columns and arches, once the central place before the entrance into the emperor's quarters, the ground-floor of the southern façade, colloquially known as "Diocletean's cellars" which in reality is a substructure for the area on the upper floor. As the terrain on which the palace was built perceptibly sloped toward the sea, the ground-floor construction served for leveling the space of the palace. Throughout the centuries the upper, emperor's floor has been almost totally destroyed so that these ground-floor architectural constructions are an excellent guide to the space of the emperor's residence. The monumental octagonal edifice of the emperor's mausoleum along the eastern wing of the Peristyle has been well pre-

expanded because of its growing role as a trade juncture in traffic with the continent. With some specific episodes, Split shared the fate of the rest of Dalmatian space. Due to rapid industrialization after WWII, a large influx of population took place so that the city extensively expanded onto areas significantly distant from its historical core in which are located most of its artistic monuments of exceptional significance.

In accordance with international conventions in 1979 UNESCO included the historical center of Split with its Diocletian's palace into the register of world heritage. As the best preserved example of antique imperial palaces in the world it is considered the key building for knowing this kind of architecture. In addition, the influence of the Split palace on the development of urbanism and construction within the European context is exceptionally significant.

The complex of Diocletian's palace has the shape of a

*Right: Split, three civilizations on Peristyle.
Old Egypt sphinx, Roman arches, the Romanesque
bell-tower of Split cathedral in the background*

Split cathedral, altar of St. Domnius,
by Bonino of Milan, 1427

Split cathedral, the altar of St. Stasius,
by Juraj Dalmatinac, 1448

served primarily owing to the circumstance that shortly after the Salone refugees settled in it began to serve as a cathedral onto which at the end of the 13th century a high late-Romanesque belfry was built. Because the altars of Solin saints martyrs are in the church, despite the fact that it was consecrated to the Virgin Mary, from earliest times it has been called the church of St. Duima, the first Solin bishop martyr.

The historical core of Split has preserved a large number of Romanesque, late Gothic, Renaissance and Baroque palaces belonging to famous Split noble families. Some of the most important artists of the time such as Juraj Dalmatinac,

Left: Juraj Dalmatinac, scene of Christ's scourging, detail from the altar of St. Stasius, 1448

Right: Split, the northern, "Golden gate", the main entrance into Diocletian's palace

Baptismal fount shaped like a cross in the baptistery of the Split cathedral. In the foreground a plate with the image of a Croatian ruler from the 11th century

*Left and above: Split, the courtyard of the large Papalić palace, today the Museum of
the city of Split
Scene from the National Square
Left and below: Split, the Medieval church of St. Mikula in Veli Varoš, 11th century
Split, church of the Holy Trinity, 8th-9th century*

*Above: Split, Ivan Meštrović, the
sculpture of bishop Grgur of Nin
from 1929*

Split, Museum of Croatian Archeological Monuments.
The central space with the ciborium of early Medieval
Croatian churches

Split, Archeological Museum, Roman mosaic from Salona

Split, porch of the Meštrović Gallery

Ivan Meštrović:
Portrait of Olga Meštrović, Split, Meštrović Gallery

Andrija Alešija and Nicholas of Florence worked on these buildings. Important monasteries are to be found around the city center. Modern times have left their artistic seal on Split. Of the numerous historicist buildings mention should be made of the famous Prokurative which close off the western part of the famous and exceptionally picturesque Split waterfront. The great Croatian sculptor Ivan Meštrović, along with his summer house, transformed into a gallery, and the nearby citadel, bequeathed to Split some of his monumental sculptures of which the most monumental is the sculpture of bishop Grgur Ninski now standing north of the "Golden gates" of Diocletian's palace.

Today Split is an outstanding center of culture, art and science. With a number of museums and galleries that have national relevance, the theatre opera and drama, its rich publishing activities, its lively artistic life, its libraries, archives, national institutes and especially with its University, Split is today one of the strongholds of Croatian culture.

Of no lesser significance is Split's contribution to Croatian sport in many disciplines but particularly in football, basketball, tennis and water sports. Split definitely has, architectonically speaking, the most beautiful football stadium in Croatia, the home ground of the famous football club "Hajduk" which was designed by B. Magaš in 1979.

Poljica

The extraordinarily impressive massif of the lonely mountain Mosor stretches for 25 kilometers to the east of Split, from the mouth of the river Žrnovica to where the river Cetina merges with the sea. The villages on both side of the mountain, including those along the coast go by the common name Poljica. They are customarily divided into Upper Poljica (Zamosorska) which lie on the land side of the mountain chain, Middle Poljica (Završka) which stretch out in the valley between Mosor and the long mountain slope Poljička Gora and Lower Poljica (Primorska) along the seashore from Stobreč to Omiš. The interesting political phenomenon of the Poljica principality, frequently called "Poljica Republic" is associated with the history of this area and its proud inhabitants. This was a wholly original Medieval community consisting of 12 village districts, a kind of "peasant republic" which gained its autonomy as far back as the 11th century within the framework of the Croatian Medieval state. The structure of the Poljica principality was codified in the Poljica statute whose earliest core derives from the beginning of the 15th century. Together with the century and a half older Vinodol Book of Law the Poljica statute is one of the most significant and interesting Croatian historical-legal monuments.

Omiš

The city of Omiš stands at the very mouth of the river Cetina. Its significant strategic location called for a construction of a settlement already in Antiquity. Thusly during the Roman period there was here the settlement Oneum. In the 10th century, on the right side of the river in Priko the pre-Romanesque church of St. Peter was built which has been completely preserved up to our own days. The urban structure of Omiš itself

Omiš, the church of St. Peter in Priko, 9th-11th century

The river Cetina at its river-mouth nearby Omiš

dates back to the Middle Ages. The walls from that period were destroyed in the 19th century except for a smaller part on the southern side and the tower of Peovica (Mirabela) over the city on the Babnjača slope. Peovica is without doubt the most typical preserved Romanesque fortification in Dalmatia (13th century). Next to the Baroque parish church stands a small but picturesque Baroque square. A series of houses from the 16th and the 17th century lie along the main street.

Radman's mills, surrounded by enormous plane-trees and a fishpond, are located upriver on the Cetina. Today this is a famous and favorite popular resort for the middle Dalmatian region.

The Cetina river region

The continental part of Dalmatia, the hinterland of the conglomerate of coastal settlements and cities from Togir to Omiš with Split at its center, is geographically marked by the massifs of the mountains of Dinara and Svilaja and by the flow of the river Cetina which in a wide loop makes its way to the sea near Omiš. The Cetina springs from a lake which is located 380 meters above sea level and two kilometers to the north of Vrlika, then after flowing through the valley fields it finds its way through a series of steep and picturesque canyons around the massif of the Mosor mountain to its mouth nearby Omiš.

For thousands of years this area was a border, even a bulwark between the continent and the Mediterranean world, its specific civilization and customs. The impressive Karst landscape of the Dalmatian hinterland is particularly marked by the flow of the Cetina river which makes its way through a long valley forming picturesque Karst fields such as the Cetina one, the Vrlik, Hrvatac and Sinj one. A part of the valley is today under the water of the artificial lake created by the damn of the large hydro-electrical plant Peruča.

Sinj

The center of the Cetina river region is the city of Sinj. In Roman times, the Delmatian settlement Osinium stood on the hillsides where stands the city of Sinj. This is where the name

Sinj, the image of the famous Our Lady of Sinj within a silver frame, 18th century

Sinj, Alka participants

Alka contestant in full gallop

Left: The equipment of the Alka participants　　　　　　　　　　　　　*Source of the Cetina river*

derives from. In the Middle Ages it became the seat of the Knin duke Ivan Nelipčić as a gift bestowed by the Hungarian-Croatian king Louis I. Angevine. Soon after the fall of Bosnia, already at the beginning of the 16th century, the whole area of Sinj was in Turkish hands. The Turks lost Sinj in 1698 but being a strategically important stronghold they tried to retake it in 1715 sending a powerful army under the walls (according to sources there were 40.000 to 60.000 soldiers). Its 700 defenders succeeded in defending the city on the feast of the Assumption when the defeated Turkish army gave up the siege. The people of Sinj explained the victory as a miracle done on their behalf by the Virgin and vowed to stage a knightly tournament every first Sunday in August, the famous Sinjska alka.

The vow of the knights of Sinj has been preserved up to our days and Sinjska alka has not only become the most important event in the entire Cetina region but with its successful heeding of tradition, its strict rules, picturesque ceremonies in original uniforms and the attractiveness of the tournament itself, it has become a cultural event of national significance. The competition of the Sinj knights dressed in uniforms from the beginning of the 18th century consists of hit-

The church of the Holy Salvation at the source
of the river Cetina

Makarska under the Biokovo massif

ting the alka, two small concentric iron rings connected with forks. The alka is hung at a height of 3,22 meters and the horseman has to hit it with a spear while at full gallop. In addition to the contest itself, what impresses the viewers is the Alka procession of knights and their boys at whose head is the war lord in a sumptuous uniform.

During the formation of the old Croatian kingdom, at the source of the river Cetina, nearby today's village Cetina was located the seat of the Vrhrik parish. The remnants of the church of the Holy Salvation, which in the 9th century was raised by the Cetina district prefect Gastika, have here been preserved in good measure. According to its building concept this is one of the most interesting pre-Romanesque edifices in the area which at this period were being settled by Croats.

The Makarska littoral

The Makarska littoral is 60 kilometers long, stretching from Vrulje bay in the northwest to the region of Baćine, that is cape Višnjica in front of the port of Ploče in the southeast,

almost to the place where the river Neretva flows into the sea. Towards the hinterland it is encircled by the mighty mountain massif Biokovo while seaward it opens to the Brač, Hvar and Neretva canals. Docile bays and long pebbly beaches, the thick, variegated and rich vegetation wherein have developed picturesque settlements along the seacoast and older villages over them seems to recline at the bottom of some gigantic Antique theatre whose steep half-circle is composed of the craggy heights and ash-gray cliffs of Biokovo mountain whose heights, towering over two kilometers (Saint George's peak – 1764 meters), can in their entirety be viewed from sea level. With its inter-permeation but also state of tension between the docile shore of Mediterranean vitality and the powerful expression of monumental Karst heights, as well as the demure yet harmonious products of human hands, the Makarska region is without doubt one of the most impressive parts of the Croatian Adriatic sea.

Today the city of Makarska is one of the most developed tourist centers within the region of central Dalmatia. It is situated under a mountain in a sheltered bay which is enclosed by two smaller peninsulas, the peninsula of St. Peter and the

Makarska, the main square with a statue of the friar Andrija Kačić Miošić, the work of the sculptor Ivan Rendić

Osejava peninsula, almost in the middle of the littoral at whose back stands the Biokovo mountain massif. According to the logic of its geographical location it was deemed important as far back as Antiquity. During the Middle Ages it was under the rule of Hungarian-Croatian and afterwards of Bosn-ian rulers. At the end of the 15th century it fell under the rule of the Ottomans. After 150 years Makarska was liberated from Turkish rule and during the Venetian administration it renovated its urban structure. During the Austrian period, as one of the first public sculptures in Croatia the sculptor Ivan

Brist

Franciscan monastery in Zaostrog

Modro jezero (blue lake) nearby Imotski

Rendić made a statue of the famous Croatian poet and collector of Croatian folk literary traditions, the Franciscan friar Andrija Kačić Miošić. The Franciscan monastery was renovated in the 17ᵗʰ century. Today, along with its archive and library, a section of the monastery has been turned into the Malacological Museum, a unique collection of shells and sea snails from all continents. The distinctive features of the Biokovo Karst terrain, the variegated nature of its morphology as well as the specific Karst and Mediterranean flora with numerous endemic species, which have been a subject of study during the last two centuries, contributed to the decision made in 1981 to proclaim the wider Biokovo massif, encompassing around 20.000 hectares, the Biokovo Park of nature with all indications that this exceptional preserve of nature will soon receive the status of a national park.

A number of picturesque settlements which, despite widespread construction of tourist facilities, have managed more or less to preserve the complexes of their original rural architecture. Makarska Riviera as far as tourism goes is one of the most important parts of the Croatian coast.

Beyond the Biokovo mountain massif

In the Dalmatian hinterland, behind the Biokovo mountain chain, towards the border with Bosnia and Herzegovina, lies the region of the town of Imotski. This area was inhabited as early as the early Iron Age while during Antiquity an important Roman road passed through here from Salona to the city of Narona in the Neretva valley. During the Middle Ages the city was the possession of the Croatian state, later under the rule of the Nemanjić Bosnian nobles, and then under the Hungarian-Croatian kings. Numerous, richly decorated in relief standing tomb-stones have been preserved here from the Medieval period. Turkish incursions spread to this area very early and Imotski, a market place and a small town, came under Venetian rule in 1718.

It is within the Imotski region that the folk ballad about Hasanagica was composed in the 16ᵗʰ century, an extraordinary work of folk literature which was incorporated by Herder into the anthology of European folk poetry and which was translated by Goethe into German.

In the immediate vicinity of Imotski are Modro and Crveno jezero (Blue and Red Lakes), interesting Krast phenomena, especially the Red one whose depth is over 300 meters (its name derives from the reddish stones which encircle it). In 1969 it was declared a geo-morphological monument of nature.

To the southeast of Imotski lies Vrgorac, once a border town where one of the most famous and best Croatian poets, Tin Ujević was born in 1891.

Central Dalmatian islands

A chain of large inhabited islands which significantly contribute to the morphological wealth and beauty of the Dalmatian coast stand in front of the coast of middle Dalmatia.

Island of Šolta

The westernmost is Šolta which because of its proximity to the Split region had fortified summer houses of the Split noble families. The settlements were founded by peasants-serfs who worked the fields of the Split owners.

Island of Brač

As far as its area goes, Brač is the largest Dalmatian island, while the peak of Vidova gora, 778 in height, is the tallest peak of any Croatian island. Between Šolta and Brač is the sea passageway called Splitska vrata (Split gate). According to onomasticists, the name of the island derives from the deer, a cult animal which in the Illyrian language is called brenton. Brač is an island with a larger number of settlements of which most are on the northern side of the island facing the land. This is due to the logic of the perennial contact between the island and the land but also because of the numerous historical migrations which brought to the island refugees from the coast. As Brač is a significant stone quarrying center, where high-quality stone is collected from the quarries on the island, it needs to be emphasized that in all the Brač settlements, even when rural buildings are in question, there exists a certain culture in building in stone.

From 1827 up to the present day Supetar has remained the administrative center of the island so that buildings raised in the spirit of different neo-styles from the 19th century encircle

Blaca desert on the island of Brač

Above: Bol on the island of Brač

Right: Starigrad on the island of Hvar, the fish-pond in Petar Hektorović's Tvrdalj

a fine stone pier. Sutivan, stretched out around a smallish port, gathers together the complexes of noble summer houses amongst which the fortified summer house of the poet Jerolim Kavanjin is particularly important. In Bobovišća, in a deep quiet bay, stands the Renaissance-Baroque complex of the Gligo family. The famous Croatian poet Vladimir Nazor was born in Postire. Not far from Pučišća is located the large Vaselje quarry where numerous generations of stone-cutters and masons have been trained. Amongst these were the famous Bokanići people but also the sculptors Branislav Dešković and Valeria Michieli.

Selca dominates over the eastern part of the island and is one of the centers of Brač stone-cutting. A row of statues which during the 20th century have been raised in the center of the settlement to honor famous Croatian and world figures represent a special attraction.

Bol is the only settlement situated on the southern side of the island. Of the early Christian and Medieval registered edifices, one ought to mention the Dominican monastery of Our Lady of Mercy raised in 1475. The church was expanded in 1636, while alongside the monastery there stands a museum with many valuable items, a numismatic collection, manuscripts, incunabulums and works of art. Zlatni rat (Golden cape) is the outstanding locality of Bol. This is a strip of golden yellow pebbles more than 700 meters long which changes its shape depending on the sea-currents. To the west of Bol is the renowned Pustinja Blaca (Blaca Desert) which came into being in the 16th century when two Glagolithic priests found their ascetic dwelling in Ljubitovica cave. A hermit's monastery quickly developed here which grew in the 18th and the 19th century. Thanks to a library collection of 11,000 books, its archive and numerous instruments amongst which a large telescope should be emphasized, many of the hermits did science.

Island of Hvar

Hvar is the longest of the Adriatic islands. The original Greek name of the island was probably Paros after the island from which came the Greek settlers. Later the name was changed to Pharos after the much more famous island situat-

Left: Hvar, city-loggia and the watchtower　　　　　　　　　　　　　*Above: Hvar, the main square with the cathedral*

ed in front of Alexandria. The Romans called it Pharia while the Dalmatian Roman appellation was Fara out of which the Croats created Hvar. Settled in pre-history Hvar shared the destiny of the Dalmatian region. The history of Hvar records the famous folk uprising which in 1510 was led by Matija Ivanić against the local nobility and which was put down in blood by the Venetians. Of interest is the fact that because of its exceptional climate as early as 1868 the so-called Hygienic society was founded indicating the emergence of a new kind of prosperity on Hvar – tourism.

The main settlement of the island is the city of Hvar, a place with a long history and an abundance of historical and artistic monuments. The main city square, the Hvar Pijaca is an exceptionally comely and urbanistically functional site directly connected to the waterfront. The late Renaissance Hvar cathedral and the city loggia entirely renovated during

the same period are two of the prominent buildings. The south side of the square is closed off by the large building of the Arsenal, on whose first floor as early as 1612 the first municipal theatre in Europe was built. Today the city of Hvar is one of the leading Croatian tourist centers with a large hotel complex. Directly in front of the bay of Hvar harbor lies the miniature but attractive archipelago Pakleni otoci.

On the western side of the island in a deep cove of Starigrad bay stands Starigrad. Starigrad developed from the Greek colony of Pharos. The colony was encircled with walls whose remains have been preserved. The antique agricultural space of the Starigrad field has also been preserved and this is an archeological rarity. In the center of the city stands the fortified summer house , Tvrdalj Petra Hektorovića, with a fish-pond and a park built around 1520. Amongst the numerous Hvar settlements Jelsa stands out. It is located in a pic-

turesque bay on the northern side of the island where tourism began to develop even before WWI. In nearby Vrbovska of particular interest is the Renaissance church of St. Mary altered into a church-fortress in 1580 which was a relatively rare phenomenon even during those turbulent times.

Island of Vis

Vis is the most distant of the Croatian islands. The island rises high into the air and it has three mountain chains with peaks that reach up to 600 meters. In the third millennium B.C., an old people of Mediterranean origin lived on the island of Vis. At the end of the second millennium these were driven away by the Illyrians while Greeks from Syracause in the 4th century B.C. founded on Vis their central Adriatic colony – Issa. Standing alone almost in the middle of the Adriatic Vis has throughout its history had an exceptional strategic significance. The possibility of controlling the central and northern Adriatic made it the target of many conquerors so that almost to our own days it has been fortified as an Adriatic fortress. Of the numerous naval military encounters without doubt the most significant is the 1866 battle nearby Vis when the Austrian imperial fleet defeated the more numerous Italian war navy.

The island is characterized by exceptional natural attractions while two of its larger settlements stand out: the city of Vis which lies in a deep cove on the northern part of the island and the important fishing settlement Komiža located in a cove under the hill Hum to the west.

Five nautical miles distant from Komiža lies the island of Biševo on whose eastern side is the famous Modra špilja (Blue cave) one of the most famous Adriatic natural attractions.

Island of Vis, the city of Vis

Komiža, the church of St. Nicholas, one-time Benedictine monastery

Island of Biševo nearby Vis, Blue cave

Island of Korčula

Korčula is one of largest and the most thickly populated of the Croatian islands. Its name derives from the Greek Corcyra Melaine – Black Korčula which is related to the dark color of the island, overgrown as it is with pines and cypress trees. The most significant settlement on the island is the city of Korčula, an eminently Mediterranean historical city with an excellently preserved urban core, fortresses, palaces, town hall and religious buildings. Renowned for their stone-cutting skills which they proved in numerous monuments from Zadar to Dubrovnik, the master stonemasons of Korčula embellished the monuments of their city, especially its Renaissance prince's castle, the town hall, the loggia and the Korčula cathedral.

Right: Korčula, the folk game Moreška
in front of the cathedral of St. Mark

Above:
Motif from Vela Luka

Left:
Korčula, the square in front of the town-hall

The island of Korčula is a wine-growing district especially on the localities of Čar and Smokvica where some of the finest Dalmatian wines are produced. The northwestern part of the island is dominated by the large village Blato with a series of valuable complexes of houses and citadels. Vela Luka is located in a deep bay on the westernmost part of the island. The settlement developed during the 18th and the 19th century.

The Neretva river valley

On the land side of Dalmatia, opposite to the middle Dalmatian island cluster, the Makarska littoral is transformed into the broad area of the delta of the Neretva river. This is the longest river which flows into the Adriatic sea on its eastern coast. It is 218 kilometers long. Making its way in a winding course amongst the Herzegovina mountain it gradually opens up onto a broad fertile valley which is in large part located within the Republic of Croatia. The broad are of the Neretva river delta consists of twelve backwaters, eight lakes and numerous canals. Although the area is periodically inundated and swampy it has attracted settlers since Antiquity both because of its fertile fields and its rich fisheries, especially eels and white mullets.

From the northwestern rim of the Neretva delta one enters through a canal the harbor Ploče, the newest city on the Croatian shore of the Adriatic. The building of the harbor and the settlement began in 1937 to meet the need of establishing maritime and railway communication through the Neretva valley with the continental area. Nearby Ploče are the Baćinska jezera (lakes) with an abundant supply of fish and habitats of water birds. Upriver on the Neretva river lies Opuzen, once an important market place of the Dubrovnik Republic and today the center of Neretva agricultural production. Twenty two kilometers from where the Neretva river flows into the sea, at the end of its flow, lies Metković, the center of

The Neretva river valley

Neretva mandarin oranges

the entire area of the Neretva delta. The name of the settlement was mentioned in the 15th century and its importance as a market-place and harbor grew in time as a border place between the Venetian and afterwards the Austrian imperial territories and the interior of the Turkish empire. Today, on the very border between the Republic of Bosnia and Herzegovina, Metković is important in a similar manner. Hardly a few kilometers to the northwest of Metković, on the Norin, a tributary of the Neretva river, lies the village Vid on whose territory stood the famous Narona, an important and significant Roman city center. Archeological excavations have located significant buildings and entire urban complexes while in 1995 an extraordinarily important finding was discovered – Augusteum, a temple dedicated to the cult of the emperor next to which were found sixteen first class stone sculptures of more than natural dimensions.

Veliki Ston and a salt-work

Pelješac peninsula

At one time the territory of the Dubrovnik Republic, which during the first half of the 14th century also controlled the Pelješac peninsula, began at the isthmus of Ston. After Istria, going by its surface area (348 square miles) it is the largest peninsula on the Croatian coast. It is almost 62 kilometers long. Its configuration is characterized by high hills among which lie sloping fields, ideal places for abundant and high quality grapes. It is here that earlier historical settlements arose while, particularly in the 19th century, the trade in wine and a developed maritime industry contributed to the development of the littoral settlements in the sheltered bays. The main strategic interest of the Dubrovnik republic in the Pelješac area were the large salt works built in the shallow bay at the bottom of Ston canal. At times profits made on salt reached two thirds of the entire earnings of the Republic. In order to protect this production, the people of Dubrovnik, as early as 1333, founded and built according to plan the city

Ston, the second city in the Republic. The city as a whole consists of Veliki Ston which lies immediately next to the salt-licks and Mali Stom on the opposite side of the isthmus, or rather the harbor turned to the Neretva area because the salt was exported to Bosnia. The complex fortifications of Ston which played such a decisive part in defending one of the main sources of power of the Dubrovnik Republic are thought to be one of the most powerful defensive systems in this part of Europe. Substantial shell beds are located at the bottom of Mali Ston canal, especially oysters so that Mali Ston has today become a renowned gastronomic locality. One of the most picturesque landscapes of the southern Dalmatian region are found on the south side of the peninsula. The most famous wine-growing area on Pelješac stretches out to the northwest of the village Janjina. The grapes which yield the best Dalmatian wines are raised within the area encompassed by the settlements of Trtenik, Pljavčino, Potomje and Podobuče. On a steep, sunny shore, in an area called Dingač, high over the sea, on sandy terrain the plavac mali type of

Orebić beneath Sveti Ilija mountain

Attire from Orebić on Pelješac, head-covering

vine is raised which, because of the specific environment and insolation, yields the famous thick, red dingač, the most famous and finest of the Dalmatian wines. On the southern side of the peninsula stands Orebić, the center of the famous 18th and 19th century Pelješac shipping trade and today a well-known tourist destination. In the interior of the peninsula, on a wine-producing elevation above the hill Rota stands Kuna while on the northern shore of Pelješac stands the town of Trpanj, today a well-know health spa.

Southern Dalmatia

Southern Dalmatia has a number of inhabited islands some of which fascinate with their beauty.

Island of Lastovo, Lastovo, parish church of St. Kuzma and Damjan

Island of Lastovo

The most distant is Lastovo, a high island with steep shores but with beautiful deep coves. The island is for the most part covered with lush vegetation. The most important settlement is Lastovo which rises onto a slope of a Karst field, The place has retained its original picturesque quality and a large number of Gothic, Renaissance and Baroque houses.

Island of Mljet

Mljet is a relatively large island totally covered with luxuriant vegetation, to the west with pines and jasmine while to the east there are mostly stone pines. On the northwestern part there are two lakes, Veliko (Large) and Malo (Small) which are connected by a canal. On the Large lake is a small island on which stands the Benedictine monastery of St. Mary from the 12th century. The monastery church is a valuable example of Romanesque architecture. The western part of the island with the Large and Small lake has been proclaimed a national park. A large late Antiquity fortified summer-house from the 5th century has been very well preserved in the harbor Polače.

Elafite islands

A group of islands which are divided from the land by the Koločep canal are located in front of the Dubrovnik littoral. The islands of Jakljan, Šipan, Lopud, Koločep and Daksa as well as a number of smaller ones are known as the Elafite or

202

Left: Mljet, Saplunara bay   *Above: Island of Šipan, Šipan harbor*

the Jelenski islands. The name definitely derives from the Greek. Lush Mediterranan vegetation and raised agrums are typical for the inhabited islands Šipan, Lopud and Koločep. These are places where the Dubrovnik gentry had their summer houses and built residences. The islands have numerous other monuments such as Medieval churches and monasteries. These islands are constituent parts of a truly extraordinary whole that was created during the time of the Dubrovnik Republic both on the land, along the short course of Rijeka Dubrovačka, and on the indented shore next to the city of Dubrovnik itself.

The Dubrovnik littoral

The Dubovnik littoral encompasses the narrow coastal strip from Ston to Rijeka Dubrovačka. The mountain massif of the Dinara mountains which run in three parallel ranges, rising towards the hinterland, are a natural border between the littoral and Herzegovina. At the same time this is a weather and anthropo-geographic border between the Dubrovnik littoral and its hinterland. The climatic conditions of the area provide the conditions for the growth of a pronounced Mediterranean vegetation which in the coastal belt is extraor-dinarily luxuriant and variegated. This is also the result of the powerful influence of the human factor which throughout the centuries cultivated, afforested and worked the natural environment. It is precisely this conjunction of natural luxuriance and a centuries-old active relationship of the population that has made the landscape extraordinary in the sense of richness, beauty and the density of the vegetation. Besides the autochthonous Mediterranean species of flora, the Dubrovnik region abounds in samples of sub-tropic but also of continental flora which was cultivated in the numerous gardens and aboretums of the Dubrovnik summer-houses dispersed throughout the Dubrovnik littoral and the islands. The numerous plantations of lemons, oranges as well as various palms and agaves give to the broader Dubrovnik area a specific charm. Throughout the centuries, numerous sailors brought to the Dubrovnik region many tropical and sub-tropical plants and trees from their distant voyages.

The extraordinarily variegated geomorphology of the Dubrovnik region – including its shady, steep coast, its deep bays, sandy beaches, smaller fertile fields, relatively high hills which in places reach all the way to the sea, the numerous islands, uninhabited islets and crags, along with the extraordinary wealth and luxuriance of the vegetation as well as the exceptional clarity of the spacious seas – makes this

region particularly attractive. The cultivation of space has continued here for centuries. It is as though human endeavor and nature went hand in hand , intertwining natural beauty, architectonic complexes and horticultural interventions. The result of this fortunate connection is one of the most beautiful and most impressive spaces not only on the Croatian coast and the entire Adriatic area but also one of the most cultivated oasis on the Mediterranean.

The settlements on the Dubrovnik littoral, Slano, Trsteno, Veliki and Mali Zaton are authentic examples of this link. An outstanding example for this is Trsteno famous for the brilliant Gothic-Renaissance summer-house of the Gučetić (Gozze) family and the gardens that surround it. The arboretum abounds in numerous exotic plants and has a cultivated architectonic frame. In 1736, the Baroque Neptune's fountain was raised with a small lake and an artificial cave up to which an aquedact was constructed. The Gučetić summer-house is also well known for the gatherings of the Dubrovnik cultural elite of former times which were presided over by the beautiful, educated and talented Dubrovnik woman Cvijeta Zuzorić. Two gigantic plane trees planted around 1500 stand in the town's square.

Immediately in front of the entrance into the Dubrovnik northwestern harbor Gruž is a 5 kilometers deep and ranging from 200 to 400 meters wide bay which in reality is the flooded mouth of the river Ombla. Since as late as the Middle Ages this place was still designated Rijeka (river), the bay is called Rijeka Dubrovačka. Protected by the vicinity of the city, navigable along its whole length, with an abundance of drinking water, it was an almost ideal place for the building of summer-houses by the Dubrovnik nobility. A large number of summer houses were built in the 16th century in the Gothic-Renaissance and the Renaissance style.

Dubrovnik

The city of Dubrovnik is Croatia's southernmost city. It is the cultural and educational center of the broader southern Dalmatian region. In history it is known as the central location of the famous Dubrovnik Republic, one of the smallest but without a doubt one of the most significant Mediterranean maritime-merchant states which in the period from the 14th to the 17th century played an important role as the link between eastern trade routes and the West, not only for the Adriatic area but in the eastern and the southern part of the Mediterranean.

As is very common in old Mediterranean cities, the beginnings of the city are covered by a veil of legends. Nevertheless, it is most probable that its beginnings are connected to the flight of the inhabitants of Epidaura (today Cavtat), first a Greek and later a Roman center, which the Avar-Slav invasion devastated at the dawn of the Middle Ages. Some of the survivors must have found shelter on a small, rocky but, apparently, already inhabited island of Laus. In time this place merged together with the settlement of Croats on the shore which because of the wood of Mediterranean oak (dubrava) was called Dubrovnik. The connection between the two settlements developed and the mixing of the Romanic and the Croatian population got under way. Because of alluvium, the sea strait became more and more shallow and narrow so that finally in the 11th century it was filled in. At the point where the island was joined to the shore today is to be found the widest and the most famous Dubrovnik street – Placa (Stradun). In the 12th century the settlements integrated, defending themselves by a unique system of defensive walls. In the 12th century Dubrovnik already had a developed maritime industry and trade ensuring for itself the status of the main trade emporium for the neighboring Balkan countries. As a typical Medieval Adriatic municipality throughout its history it recognized the domination of a number of powers but from the 16th century it became independent and began to call itself RESPUBLICA RAGUSINA (the Dubrovnik Republic).

Left:
Trsteno, Neptune's fountain in the garden of the
Gučetić summer house

Right:
Dubrovnik, the western entrance into the city - gates of Pila,
around 1537

Dubrovnik, Minčeta tower and a series of powerful fortifications defend the city from the land

The period from the 15th to the 16th century is commonly labeled "the Golden Age" of the Dubrovnik Republic. During this period the city experienced its greatest economic boom especially in trade, in the production of textiles and salt and in ship-building. This material prosperity was especially reflected in the construction and artistic furnishing of numerous buildings but also in the flowering of its own school of art, the creation of an authentic culture, in education and in science.

The most tragic event that befell Dubrovnik during its entire history was the catastrophic earthquake which occurred on April 6, 1667. More than 5.000 inhabitants were killed amidst the destruction of their city. One of the most

Dubrovnik, the Big Onofrio's Fountain

Dubrovnik, the church of the Holy Salvation and the monastery of the Friars Minor

Dubrovnik, the Franciscan pharmacy, one of the oldest in the world

beautiful and well-proportioned cities on the Mediterranean was demolished and subsequently totally ravaged in fires which raged through the city for days. The city was gradually rebuilt in the Baroque style, the architecture of the epoch. But even with such fundamental changes in its appearance Dubrovnik remained one of the most beautiful and urbanistically integral cities on the Mediterranean.

The thing that best characterizes the appearance of the historical core of Dubrovnik is the ring of its walls which protectively envelop its urban tissue, tying it into a dense and easy-to-view entity. This complex artifice is one of the most impressive and most powerful fortification systems on the Mediterranean. It consists of a series of forts, bastions, casements, towers and separate fortresses. The ones that particularly stand out are the fortress of St. John, Bokar and Minčeta as well as the self-standing fortresses of Lovrijenac and Revelin. The eastern Gate of Ploče and the western Gate Pila are particularly well preserved. The interior distribution of buildings within the historical city is determined by the wide longitudinal street Placa which came into being by the filling

Dubrovnik, cloister of the Franciscan monastery

in of the once narrow sea canal. The Placa is the main city thoroughfare dividing the city into its southern and northern part. At its western tip, immediately near the gate of Pila, the Placa broadens into a smaller square which is surrounded by the Renaissance church of the Holy Salvation, the convent of the Poor Clares and to the north the famous Franciscan monastery, renowned for its brilliant artworks, books and archival material as well as for one of the oldest preserved European pharmacies. The Large Onofrij's fountain stands in the middle of the square. The builder from Naples, Onofrio della Cava, who was also the designer of the first Dubrovnik water-works, built it in 1438.

The Placa got its present appearance after the great earth-quake when the city was being quickly renovated. The variety and the picturesque nature of the one-time palaces were replaced by planned and uniform construction of Baroque houses of identical height and a similar disposition of the facades. Despite the modesty of this new architecture, one cannot deny that the whole complex possesses a harmony and a rhythm of volume as well as the dignity of pure stone surfaces.

The Onofrij's Small fountain, 15th century

The eastern expansion of Placa is the square known as Luža which was once the area of the market place. Surrounded by significant buildings, today it offers an ideal place for large city celebrations such as the holiday of the Dubrovnik patron saint, St. Vlaho which is on February 3rd, or the opening of the Dubrovnik Summer Games in July. The southern side of the square is enclosed by the Baroque church of St. Vlaho (1715) whose exterior rich decorations stand out of the strict simplicity of buildings on the Placa. In 1882 a new town hall in the neo-Gothic style was raised in the place where once stood the Gothic palace of the Great Council. A new Dubrovnik theatre was built during this process of restoration. Alongside the building

Left and above: Dubrovnik, the church of St. Vlaho

Left and below: Dubrovnik, Roland's column (15th century)

Below: Unknown Gothic master, statue of St. Vlaho made of gilt silver from the 15th century. Detail, contemporary view of the city of Dubrovnik

Dubrovnik, the Sponza palace, beginning of the 16ᵗʰ century

Right: Atrium of the Rector's palace

of the main Guard which had an apartment for the admiral, the commander in chief, the Small Onofrij's fountain was built in 1438. It is a masterwork conjoining function and decoration.

A high and slim stone column bearing a flag and decorated with the figure of the legendary Medieval knight Orlando (Rolando) dominates the middle of the square Luža. The slim high City belfry, built in 1444, precisely on the axis of the Placa, dominates the square. On the left side of the square stands the monumental Gothic-Renaissance Sponzo, one of the most beautiful buildings in Dubrovnik. It has managed to retain its appearance up to our own days. In addition to the custom offices, the building housed the state mint of coins, the bank, the state treasury and repository and the armory. The Sponza palace brought together a number of state offices which were of exceptional importance to the Republic which in large part lived on proceeds from trade. Today the most important cultural institution of the city of Dubrovnik – the Dubrovnik Archive which, by the amount and significance of its holdings, is one of the exceptionally important archives in the world, is located in the Sponza palace.

Alongside the town hall stands the Duke's palace, one of the most significant monuments of secular architecture not only in Dubrovnik but on the whole Adriatic coast. This well-proportioned Gothic-Renaissance palace owes its present appearance to numerous and centuries-long alterations and subsequent additions that were undertaken during its turbulent history.

The Dubrovnik cathedral of the Ascension of Mary has stood, as its shaped now, since the beginning of the 18ᵗʰ century. It was built after the near total destruction of the earlier Romanesque cathedral from the 12ᵗʰ-14ᵗʰ century in the 1667 catastrophic earthquake. To the west of the cathedral lies a relatively spacious and picturesque square – Gundulićeva poljana. Surrounded by numerous old stone houses, during the day this square is the boisterous, variegated and rich Dubrovnik market-place. The square is enriched by a statue devoted to the most famous of the Dubrovnik poets Ivan Gundulić, the work of the Croatian sculptor Ivan Rendić (1892).

213

Reliquary of the head of the Dubrovnik patron saint St. Vlaho in the shape of the crown of Byzantine emperors, 11th-12th century

Dubrovnik, the church of the Dominican monastery, Paolo Veneziano, Crucifix, 14th century

Župa dubrovačka and Konavle

To the southeast of the city, from cape Pelegrin to Cavtat spreads out spacious Župa bay where are located smaller settlements which are today wholly oriented towards tourism. They are part of Dubrovnik župa, the oldest possession of the city of Dubrovnik (Astarea) whose roots reach back to the 9th century. Župa is divided into Lower Župa, along the seashore, with the settlements of Kupari, Srebrno and Mlini and Upper Župa which consists of the area around the villages Brgat, Buići and Čelopci.

Cavtat

The town Cavtat (in Antiquity Epidaurum) situated on a smaller peninsula at the end of Župa bay is in reality the main harbor of the entire Konavle region. It was protected by walls which were torn down in the 19th century. Cavtat is an exceptionally harmonious Mediterranean location with comely stone houses and an abundance of greenery.

Konavle was the wheat field of the Dubrovnik Republic. Spreading to the southeast from Cavtat, up to cape Oštro on the Croatian border, this region consists of a littoral reef, the relatively broad and long Konavle field and limestone peaks of which Ilija's peak on the mountain Snježnica reaches the height of 1234 meters. The fertility of Konavle field is due to the fact that it is inundated by the waters of the subterranean rivers Konavočica, Kopačica and Ljuta and that it is watered by way of canals (from which it derives its name).

Above: Dubrovnik, the church of St. Mary on Danče, Lovro Dobričević, Madonna with the Child, poliptych from 1465

Left: Dubrovnik, the Dominican monastery, Nikola Božidarević, triptych of the Madonna with saints, around 1500

On the southern side, Gundulićeva polja is connected to the monumental Baroque flight of stairs through which one ascends to Poljana Ruđera Boškovića. The Jesuit church of St. Ignatio and the Collegium Ragusinum, the famous Dubrovnik Jesuit institution of learning, are situated here. Many maintain that this Baroque complex is not only the most Baroque corner of Dubrovnik but of the whole of Dalmatia. In the eastern part of the city, the large complex of the Dominican monastery situated itself right next to the city walls. This area is one of the richest treasuries of the cultural and artistic heritage of the city of Dubrovnik.

To the west of the historical city core of Dubrovnik spreads out the large, wooded peninsula of Lapad. In the past Lapad was an area with numerous Renaissance summer-houses of which the most famous is the summer-house of Petra Sorkočević (16th century) which stands at the very beginning of the peninsula across the way from Gruž, the new harbor of Dubrovnik.

Konavle is the border region between the republic of Croatia, Bosnia and Herzegovina and Montenegro. The littoral territory of the Republic of Croatia ends at cape Oštro.

At the very end of this short overview let us quote verses from the great Croatian poet Jure Kaštelan:

My homeland how beautiful you are and how comely
like a maiden with a water jug on her head

This simile seems to conjoin the bucolic antique spirit of the Mediterranean and the traditional aesthetics of the Croatian ethnos. Perhaps this metaphor, better than any other, grasps the very essence of the land of Croatia.

Contents